Biography of Mom Suse:
Matriarch of the Preston Area Black Communities

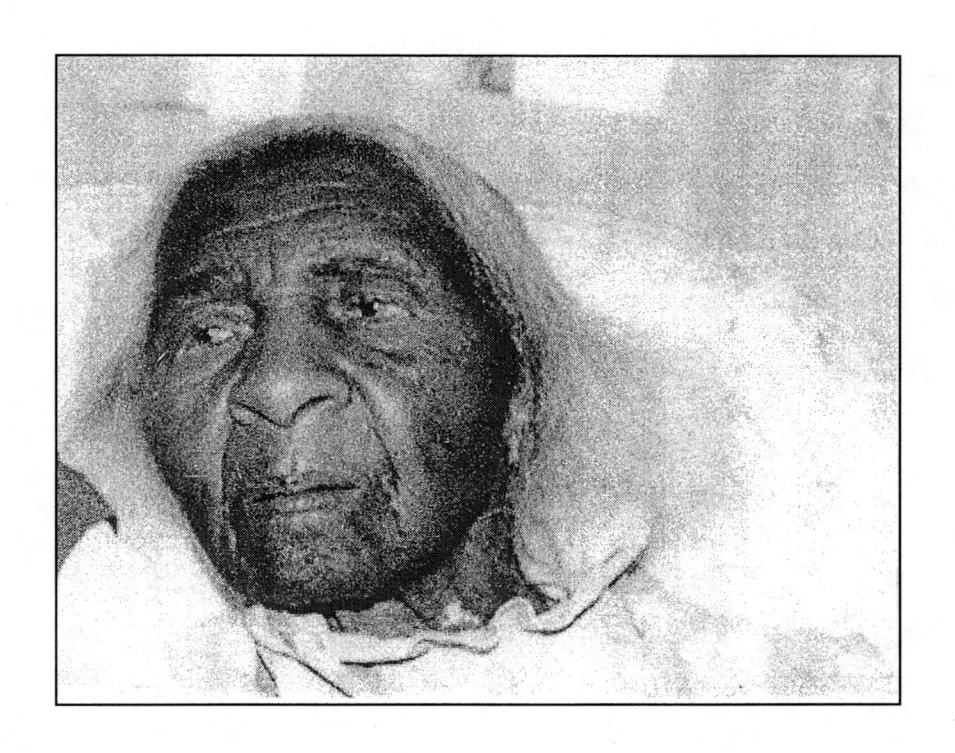

Written by: Vivian Willis

authorHOUSE®

AuthorHouse™
1663 Liberty Drive
Bloomington, IN 47403
www.authorhouse.com
Phone: 1-800-839-8640

© 2010 Vivian Willis. All rights reserved.

No part of this publication may be reproduced for public or private use, stored in a retrieval system, or transmitted, in any form or by any means, electronic, mechanical, photocopying, recording, or otherwise, without prior permission of the publisher and contributors.

First published by AuthorHouse 1/20/2010

ISBN: 978-1-4490-5201-0 (sc)
ISBN: 978-1-4490-5202-7 (hc)
ISBN: 978-1-4490-5203-4 (e)

Library of Congress Control Number: 2009912395

The copyrights for individual and organizational contributions are retained by their creators.

Map One: Mi'kma'ki (Mi'kmaq Map of the Maritimes ©1994) Native Council of Nova Scotia, Courtesy of Mi'kmaq Language Program
Map Two: Confederacy of Mainland Mi'kmaq©
Maps Three to Five: Gwen Simmonds ©2003
Map Six: The Black Cultural Centre for Nova Scotia
Photographs A: Back in Time Photos
Photographs B: 1b-3b & 5b-8b: The Black Cultural Centre for Nova Scotia
Photograph B: 4b: Frank Stanley Boyd Jr.
Photograph C: Mrs. Beatrice Jackson
Photograph D: Vivian Willis
Interview of: Mrs. Beatrice Jackson ©2003

Printed in the United States of America
Bloomington, Indiana

This book is printed on acid-free paper.

ACKNOWLEDGEMENTS

To my cousin, Gwen Simmonds researcher/editor, for her consistent source of inspiration. Her creativity continued to fuel this project. The time and energy that she expended, reached beyond the realms of duty.

Mrs. Beatrice Jackson, my Aunt, for providing her daughter Gwen with not only an interview, but numerous tidbits of the past, an era-period magazine, and a photograph of her own mother, the Late Annie V. Johnson (best friend of Mom Suse).

The Black Cultural Centre for Nova Scotia, Westphal, Nova Scotia

The Confederacy of Mainland Mi'kmaq, Millbrook, Nova Scotia

The Native Council of Nova Scotia, Truro, Nova Scotia

Back in Time Photos, Halifax, Nova Scotia

Frank Stanley Boyd Jr.

Susannah Bundy Smith
Born March 10, 1883
Died in 1988, at 105 years
8 children, 84 grand children
350 great grandchildren
10 great, great, great grandchildren

Mom Suse lived during the era of the following of major events:
End of Slavery in Nova Scotia (legally 1829-1834) (actually 1890's)
'Sinking of the Titanic' (1912),
The Asian Invasion (1914),
First World War (1914-1918),
Halifax Explosion (1917),
Great Depression (1929-39),
Second World War (1939-1945),
Viola Desmond's Civil Rights Case (1946)
Korean War (1950-1953),
Vietnam War (1964-1971),
End of Segregation in Nova Scotia (1950-1960)
Shubenacadie Indian Residential School (1922-1968)
Africville: Death of Black Community (1964 -1970)

In 1988, Mom Suse passed away peacefully, at the blessed age of 105 years. In 1883, the year of her birth, Canada was only sixteen year old and had consisted of four provinces, Ontario, Quebec, New Brunswick and Nova Scotia.

By contrast, in 1988, the year of Mom Suse's death, Canada had stretched out her arms from sea to sea by welcoming ten provinces and two territories into her passionate embrace: British Columbia, Alberta, Saskatchewan, Manitoba, Ontario, Québec, New Brunswick, Nova Scotia, Prince Edward Island, and Newfoundland. The territories are Yukon and Northwest.

In 1988, Brian Mulroney was Canada's Prime Minister. He led this magnificent country in a wonderful celebration of its one hundred and twenty-first birthday. This brief and personal account of Mom Suse's life was jam-packed with history.

Mom Suse's era of severe public restrictions and freedom created an antagonistic atmosphere for the Mi'kmaq and the black people. Yet, despite these immeasurable challenges, the two groups have transcended boundaries, by their belief, in the grace of the living God.

> In loving memory of Mom Suse

Susannah Bundy Smith

As Researcher/Editor: I must thank several individuals and organizations for their assistance in supplying me with timely information. The focus on Mi'kmaw and Black culture has been exceedingly rich, beyond all measure.

**The highest praise is rendered to ~ The Good Lord above whose love and encouragement has been my inspiration.

** Vivian Willis ~ Many thanks to my dear cousin, who believed in me, and trusted in my abilities to help her bring this project to fruition. As well, many thanks to 'Aunt Vivian' for granting me the use of her memoirs and picture, *Vivian Willis*.

**Beatrice Jackson ~ my mother who tirelessly answered questions and her quick recollection of past events. Many thanks for granting me permission to use her *interview*, and a photograph of my grandmother, the Late Annie V. (Beals) Johnson who was Mom Suse's best friend.

**To the Late Donald Simmonds ~ dear old dad, I acknowledge his sharing of information on slavery. He recounted the history of stowaways from Georgia to Nova Scotia. I honour my father for his love and respect for the Preston area.

**Thomas D. Simmons ~ my brother who networked with Bill Kinney of *Back in Time Photos*. Many thanks to Bill for granting me permission to use his photographs.

**Tesfa, Danso and Taayo ~ my three sons for their profound love and support.

**Dr. Henry Bishop ~ Curator/Director, the Black Cultural Centre for Nova Scotia for granting permission to use the map, *Historical Black Communities in Nova Scotia*, two pictures of Mom Suse, and the *Black Cultural Centre's picture brochure*.

**Frank Stanley Boyd Jr. ~ Sincere gratitude for his on-going professional advice and for the use of his picture, *Cornwallis Street United Baptist Church*.

**Sincere thanks to the Native organizations of Nova Scotia and Tim Bernard ~ Confederacy of Mainland Mi'kmaq, Millbrook for granting me permission to use the map, *28 Native Communities*.

**Grace Conrad ~ Native Council of Nova Scotia for giving me permission to use their map, *Mi'kma'ki (Mi'kmaq Map of the Maritimes* 1994©*)*.

**A special thanks goes out to Roger Hunka ~ of the Native Council, for taking the time to offer advice and to briefly council me on Mi'kmaw Culture.

**I am not able to offer enough thanks to Linda-Lee King for the unlimited and gracious use of her home office and the care & support that she extended to me.

**Pastor Pedro Graça ~ minister and dear friend at Dartmouth Seventh-day Adventist Church for his support and use of the church library and office.

Note: For further information on Mom Suse, more photographs and an interview contact:
Dr. Henry Bishop of the Black Cultural Centre for Nova Scotia

Dedicated to

The Late Mom Pauline Willis,

Trevor, Nina, LaTonia, Solea, Hasson and Aretha

Table of Contents

Introduction xiii

Chapter 1
Mi'kmaq & Blacks: Historical Overview 1

Chapter 2
Indian Reservations & Black Slavery 9

Chapter 3
Black Communities 19

Chapter 4
Great Grandparents Love Story 1840 21

Chapter 5
The Newlyweds: Mom Suse & Papa Demus 1904 31

Chapter 6
Our First Child 44

Chapter 7
Mr. Bundy's Lively Radio 57

Chapter 8
The Great Depression 60

Chapter 9
The Kerosene-Fed Fire 75

Chapter 10
Papa Demus battles Diabetes 83

Chapter 11
Air Raid Warning and the Cemetery 91

Chapter 12
Hallelujah No More War 99

Chapter 13
  Shubenacadie Indian Residential School 106

Chapter 14
  Mom Suse's Most Difficult Journey 119

Chapter 15
  The Passing of Papa Demus 133

Chapter 16
  Time for Healing & Forgiveness 145

Chapter 17
  The Grandame: 105 Years of Wisdom 150

Appendix
  Turn of the Century Clothing 164
  Maps 170
  Photographs 180
  Footnotes 195
  Bibliographies 196
  Newspapers and Articles 198

Introduction

THIS TRUE STORY IS based on the life of an amazing lady who was born in 1883. She was a dominant force, in the Preston area black communities aptly called, 'The Barrens'. Her name was Susannah Bundy Smith, but for generations, community folk simply knew her as, Mom Suse. Her path in life was set at an early age when she was taught that, "There are no bad people, only those unable to cope in dire situations".

I will touch on the truly memorable events, as well as, the tragic episodes that exemplified her character. For instance, Mom Suse had lost a total of eleven children: nine babies and two adult daughters. Thankfully, eight children would live to adulthood.

Without spiritual strength, Mom Suse would have never risen above the obstacles she encountered at the turn of the century, especially when the parochial attitude of society was mixed with the casuistic mindset of its forefathers.

The nature of this remarkable woman's soul is defined by her unwavering devotion to the higher principles, amidst the vicissitudes of life. She reciprocated God's love by serving as an excellent role model to her children, grandchildren and, indiscriminately, to all of God's children. It is interesting to note, that after living for more than a century, this self-effacing lady maintained her mental acuity. She was able to recall life's events verbatim, similar to that of an *African Griot, a highly respected person who recounts centuries of historical genealogy.

Even her staunchest critics would readily admit that her contribution to communal and family life was exemplary amidst the stark poverty of the Great Depression. Times were tough...

real tough, especially for black people whom the Nova Scotian government segregated from mainstream society and dispersed to 48 black communities.

Mom Suse married and lived in North Preston (formerly known as New Road). It would eventually become the largest and most isolated of the four Preston area communities consisting of East Preston, Cherry Brook and Lake Loon. Yet for years, Mom Suse was called the "Witch of North Preston". Perhaps, because she had an uncanny knowledge of prescience events. She did have an unshakable calm in the face of adversity. When she was surrounded by despair, her pain was accompanied with peace. Mom Suse reached for hope in the storms of life, and held the power of God in her hands.

For many years to come, Mom Suse will be remembered for her generosity and vivacity of spirit. It is hoped that this family's history will ignite a sense of pride in our most cherished possessions: the Good Lord above, family and our fellow citizens.

*Camara Laye, L'enfant noir, Maury Euroliv S.A., 1953, p.x. 1.

CHAPTER 1

IMAGE FOR A MOMENT being born in 1883, in a rural black community of Cherry Brook near Dartmouth, Nova Scotia in Eastern Canada. Now, imagine still, living for more than 100 years. At the time of Susannah Bundy's birth on March 10th, 1883, the Dominion of Canada was approaching its 16th anniversary on July 1st, 1867. This new country consisted of only four provinces: Ontario (Upper Canada), Québec (Lower Canada), New Brunswick and Nova Scotia, the smallest and most eastern.

Nova Scotia measures 55,487 km. (21,425 sq. mi.), and is connected to New Brunswick by a narrow strip of land called an isthmus. The isthmus of Chignecto is Mi'kmaw Indian for 'footcloth'. The peculiar landmass of Nova Scotia protrudes into the Atlantic Ocean. It has the form of a lobster whose claw resembles the island of Cape Breton that was connected to the mainland during the mid 1900's via the Canso Causeway.

The Bay of Fundy is the body of water that separates Nova Scotia from New Brunswick and the northeastern border of Maine, USA. The Atlantic Ocean and the Gulf Stream moderate the climate of Nova Scotia with its flow of warm water from the Tropics. Mom Suse's life was equally affected by the political and social climate of her era. Yet, she remained strong and connected, being sheltered in the religious warmth of the black community.

In the year of 1883, Canada's smallest province was jammed-packed with history. Sir John A. Macdonald (1815-1891) was the Prime Minister of the Dominion for a second term. But, more importantly, he was the Father of Confederation on July 1st, 1867, in Charlottetown, Prince Edward Island.

Vivian Willis

In order to appreciate the depth of Canada's historical impact on Mom Suse's era, it is necessary to return to the source of our intriguing provincial history. Unfortunately, we may not want to acknowledge past truth, but this truth is undeniably, the way we were.

The Mi'kmaq Indians inhabited Nova Scotia, thousands and thousands of years before the Europeans arrived. The name Mi'kmaq means, 'my kin-friends'. The Mi'kmaq were a nomadic tribe whose well-structured and simplistic lifestyle accommodated their seasonal food supply. They lived undisturbed, thus enjoying the bounties of both land and sea. Long before the institution of European-made boundaries, the original Mi'kmaq homeland extended to the southeastern Gaspé Bay peninsula of New Brunswick, which included Prince Edward Island.

Hence, the Maliseet Indians of New Brunswick were the first trading partners of the Mi'kmaw. And, at some point in time, a band of Mi'kmaq settled in St. Georges, Newfoundland, which became Canada's most eastern province in 1949.

Our First Nations saw no reason to alter the land, in any way or form. For they felt a connection to the land... an intangible bond that served them well. In the early 17th century, New Brunswick and Nova Scotia were named 'Acadia', by French explorers. The Acadians in Nova Scotia established Port Royal in 1604, as the first French settlement, north of Florida.

Through commerce with French fur traders, the Mi'kmaq had amassed European goods. The Mi'kmaq were a highly religious people who, traditionally, rendered homage to the 'Great Spirit'. Their belief in the Creator had always been their mainstay.

Yet, the French believed that the Mi'kmaq lacked direction. The French reasoned within themselves that the spiritual needs of the Natives would be better served by conversion to Christianity (Roman Catholicism). Incidentally, much of this religious conversion came about by force.

But, this was not the Mi'kmaq's only concern; the worse was yet to come. Events were soon to take place that would drastically change the life of the Mi'kmaq, forever.

Back in Europe, the disease of smallpox had continued to snuff out the lives of many. Smallpox was a highly contagious malady that disfigured its victims with scars or pockmarks. Those fortunate enough to have survived its wrath were often left permanently deaf or blind.

Unfortunately, the early pioneers brought this virus to the New World, thereby disturbing the equilibrium of the Natives. The Mi'kmaq contracted this plague that shrouded them under a blanket of death.

The next 'plague' to fiercely attack the Natives was alcohol, which they rightfully labelled, 'firewater'. The Europeans gave the Natives a lower-grade of whiskey, and it wasn't long before they were addicted to this poison. The effects were far-reaching. This poisonous liquid was transferred to the bloodstream of their innocuous children.

The following is a poignant account of the affects of alcohol even centuries later, as seen in eyes of two innocent Native children. "Lots of people think alcohol can solve their problems. Alcohol can ruin your heart – nobody can live without a heart. Please don't drink when you are pregnant. It can harm your baby. If you drink too much your [children] will drink alcohol when they are young. You will teach them a bad habit."[1]

The other innocent youth writes, "Drinking can make you crazy, it makes you think about the bad things that have happened."[2]

The pioneers, who emigrated from the British Isles, changed the province's French name of Acadia to Nova Scotia. It is Latin for "New Scotland". The official provincial welcome of "Ciad Mile Fialte," is Gaelic for "One Thousand Welcomes".

The capital City of Halifax was established in 1749, by the British commander, Lieutenant-Colonel Edward Cornwallis, complete with 2000 settlers.

Halifax was the first permanent English settlement, in Canada. It included a military and naval base to counter the threat of attack from the Acadians at Louisbourg, Cape Breton.

Halifax was soon to become the hub of commercial operations. The province would prosper through its provision of services to the British military, especially during colonial resistance. The government allotted harbour front property, and land along the eastern shore, to be donated to all military personnel.

However, Commander Cornwallis vehemently opposed the presence of First Nations people, and ordered that they be annihilated. Cornwallis decided that the scalps of Mi'kmaw men, women and children would be recompensed at ten guineas."3

The original Mi'kmaq name for Halifax is "Chebucto", which means 'great haven'. It refers to the saltwater harbour and its natural shelter, the Bedford Basin. One year later, in 1750, across from Halifax harbour, the Town of Dartmouth was established with 356 English settlers. In the following year, the British brought a large influx of Protestant pioneers to Nova Scotia from Germany, France, Switzerland, and other European countries. They were primarily settled in Lunenburg and Queens' counties.

A few years later, in 1752, the Dartmouth Ferry Service was founded to provide transportation between the harboured town and city. The Preston area black communities were located outside of Dartmouth about thirty years later. East Preston was the first area community.

In 1500, the slave trader, Gaspar Corte Real, enslaved a group of Natives. It is understood that there were a few Mi'kmaq among the group. It seems that Real's ship was wrecked in a storm, although two other ships had returned to Portugal, safely.

The first documentation of a black person to Nova Scotia was Mattieu da Costa, an ex-slave of the Portuguese. He travelled with Samuel de Champlain 1604-1606, on an expedition to Port Royal. This town was later renamed Annapolis Royal, by the British.

Mattieu served as an interpreter between the French and the Mi'kmaq Indians. At that time in history, Britain was the dominant world power. The words of her song echoed its sentiment, 'Hail Britannia! Britannia rules the waves. Britain never, ever, ever shall be slaves'. The empire would grow, quickly. In 1607, Britain began its colonization along the American eastern seaboard. These Thirteen colonies were later known as the New England states. By 1609, the extermination of the Natives in Virginia was almost complete. As well, events were soon to take place in the 'New World' that would drastically change the life of the black man, forever.

Mom Suse: Matriarch of the Preston area Black Communities

It was in 1619, that the first group of Africans were transported via slave ship to Jamestown, Virginia. Together, they were shackled in their dark tomb beneath the sea. There, in this cruel and restrained position, they laid... subjected to beatings, starvation, sickness and too often... death.

It was nothing short of a miracle that any of the slaves survived the journey or 'Middle Passage' across the Atlantic. They were suffering from multiple degrees of trauma. A hellish shock! There, they laid for more than a few months. And, to think of the profoundness of their deplorable state... the worse was yet to come!

Meanwhile, in 1638, New France (Québec), reported Canada's first slave purchase of Olivier Le Jeune. He was around six to eight years of age from Madagascar, East Africa. It is probable that he was the first African to spend the better part of his life in Canada – before obtaining his freedom. It is also noted that La Liberte, was the first black man to have lived on Cape Sable, the southeastern tip of the province.

In Lower Canada, or Québec, slavery was legalized in 1709, with a Proclamation by Jacques Randot. From 1753 to 1756, a proclamation was issued in Nova Scotia that ordered that hostilities be committed against the Mi'kmaq Indians.

One of the enslaved was a young man by the name of Olaudah Equiano (1745-1790), a native from the Ibo tribe of Nigeria. As a child, Equiano was kidnapped from the Benin region of Nigeria and transported into slavery in the states. Later, as a free man in Great Britain, Equiano wrote an autobiography. He became one of the first African authors of English literature.

By the way, Halifax, Nova Scotia was not to be excluded from this new enterprise of 'human cargo'. Documents reveal that in 1769, the Slave Trade was alive and well in Halifax; complete with a Whipping Post and Public Slave Auction at the Market Square. And when a sympathetic white man attempted to offer aid, he too, was shown *no* mercy! It appears that during the inception of Halifax, the purchasing and selling of slaves was nothing new.

The following advertisement from the Halifax Gazette of November 1, 1760, serves as a sample: "To be sold at public auction, on Monday, the 3rd of November at the house of John Rider, two slaves, viz: a boy and girl about eleven years of age: likewise a puncheon of choice old cherry brandy with sundry other articles."4

It is inconceivable to grasp the reality that human beings were utilized as slaves and advertised as human chattel. But then, truth is strange, and much more painful than fiction.

Numerous American slaves escaped from Georgia, and sought refuge on ships travelling northward to Nova Scotia. They heard that it was a land with a lot of woods. Hence, a safe place to hide from former slave masters, should they come searching.

It seems that the North American 'powers that be' were beginning to waltz with their 'lover', capitalism. In the New World, the Europeans were the first group of enslaved people. For various reasons, this venture was unsuccessful. The next race of people to be preyed upon, were the Natives. Their enslavement also proved to be unproductive, because many succumbed to sickness or escaped the intolerable treatment.

Finally, the problem was solved with African slaves. They seemed to be a tough and enduring race. However, their dark complexion and woolly hair worked against them for purposes of identification, should they not co-operate.

It must be equally noted that, the Africans were perceived as heathens or persons without a soul, without a home and, without a voice. Here, in the white man's land, they were entirely under the white man's control... problem solved! The African slave had no spokesperson in the 'New World'. Their 'voice' was already lost while in the bowels of the slave ship.

The continent of Africa is comprised of many distinct countries. There are several tribal languages within a single country.

Yet, this lack of linguistic commonality was no deterrent from slave revolts on ships. Nothing is as sweet as *freedom*! To make matters worse, upon exiting the slave ship, the Public Auction Block was the next inevitable separator.

The prosperity of the continent called the 'New World' was accomplished, in part, in an extremely large part, through the institution of slavery. Yet, one slave, is just *one*, too many!

And not believing that slavery existed in Canada or more specifically, in Nova Scotia, does little to negate the facts. From the 1700's to the 1890's this practice was a reality in Nova Scotia, although legally abolished between 1829 to 1834.

In the meantime, the British and French continued their power struggle. Eventually, the British succeeded, and from 1755 to 1762, they expelled 10,000 Acadians from the Annapolis Valley region. The British, who left no stone unturned, also demolished the beautiful Fortress at Louisbourg in Cape Breton.

The Acadians then, fled to New Brunswick, the New England states and to Louisiana where they are known as, 'Cajuns'. This horrific turn of events, is remembered as, 'Le Grand Dérangement', or the 'Great Displacement'.

They lost their homes. They lost their land. Many lost their lives. In 1763, only a fraction or 2000 Acadians returned home to Nova Scotia. The annexing of Acadian property had ensured that sufficient land would be available for purchase to European Protestant pioneers.

The Loyalists were the first large wave of English immigrants to settle in Canada. They settled in the Maritimes and in Ontario following, the War of American Independence (1775-1783). The first choice of prime land on lakefront and waterfront property was given to these settlers. Other location of property was offered at reduced rates. As well, it was not uncommon for the government to donate land to certain persons, who in turn, offered it to settlers.

The Mi'kmaq were allies with the French, although this bond did not seem to help their cause. The Natives were eventually drawn into the on-going conflict with the British, who had their own agenda for land use.

By the late 1700's the British had made life increasingly more difficult for the Mi'kmaq and, in time, the Natives were segregated and relocated to settle on, what the white man coined as, "Indian Reservations".

They lost their land. They lost their culture. Many lost their lives. At this time, the government believed assimilation would solve the 'Indian problem'. Hence, the painful forced change to Caucasian culture.

Since 1725, Treaties were drawn up as legal agreements to promote amity between the Mi'kmaq and the British. However, these reservations were strategically isolated, located in backwoods where transportation and commerce would become a challenge. Furthermore, the Natives were bound by government policy, that their homes be neither bought nor sold without government consent.

Chapter 2

More specifically, by the mid-1800 the Nova Scotian government provided for around ten reservations on the mainland followed by, at least, three more in Cape Breton: and many more would follow. In short, the Mi'kmaq were aliens in their 'native land'. For they no longer felt connected to the land. Their sense of 'oneness' had long since evaporated. Thereby, transforming itself into an endless sense of grief. For the courage of the Mi'kmaq, was stronger than defeat. But would the contentious land issue between the Mi'kmaq and the white man ever be resolved?

The concept of land ownership was unfathomable… totally foreign to the Natives. They felt a connectedness to the land, and this intangible bond had served them well. On the other hand, the white man recognized that land could be acquired 'for a price', as the only tangible method of ownership. This connection to the land would become a reality, 'by any means necessary'.

Unfortunately, the resulting actions would slowly erode the spirit of the Natives, and come to secretly haunt the spirit of the white man.

It seems that the 'powers that be' were now, seducing their lover, 'capitalism'.

Perhaps the cloak of religious and racial persecution that once clothed Europeans in the 'Old World', was wrapping itself around the Mi'kmaw and the black man in the 'New World'.

For many Europeans, life in the 'Old World' had become intolerable. When the English defeated the Scots in 1745 to 1746, the Scots were forbidden to practice their culture including the Catholic religion. In fact, the Highland Scots lost the freedom to wear their traditional kilts or even to play the bagpipes. The victors assumed that these restrictions would bring about assimilation within a period of two years.

Elsewhere in Europe, the Protestant Huguenots of France fled to North America, also upon encountering religious and racial persecution.

At the time of the Acadian Expulsion (1755-1762) and the Mi'kmaq relocation, a small number of blacks had settled in Birchtown, Shelburne, Halifax, Bridgetown, Liverpool, Amherst, Annapolis, Onslow, Cornwall and Falmouth. The first black Loyalist community was established in Birchtown.

The small community of Africville (Halifax) was in existence from 1749. The census of January 1, 1767, listed a total of 104 black Nova Scotians. In 1783, the census reported 1200 black residents.

In America, a broiling feud erupted between the British and the Americans into the War of American Independence (1775-1783). The Americans wanted independence from British rule of the Thirteen Colonies.

In the first phase of the war, the Americans signed the Declaration of Independence on July 4th, 1776. The second phase was complete when the British signed the Treaty of Paris in 1783. During the height of the war, the British retaliated in 1779 by issuing the Phillipsburgh Proclamation that enlisted the participation of free, indentured servants and slaves. These enslaved blacks were led to believe that enlistment would lead to the abolishment of slavery and ultimately, their freedom.

The first documentation of slaves settling in the rural areas of Nova Scotia did not occur until the end of the War of American Independence. Enslaved blacks arrived with their Loyalist owners in 1783-1784, although some documents identified them as 'servants'.

Similar to the Hebrew slaves in Old Testament times, blacks seemed to have thrived and survived despite all odds. For freed blacks, the equality of freedom became an illusion. They received only varying amounts of poor quality land, or none at all. Initially, several refugees died from diseases and starvation in the squalid quarters they received. Blacks realized that they had to 'fend for themselves'. They cleared land with donated and hand-made tools, planted, harvested crops and built homes on the some of the province's lowest quality soil, while many of their wives worked as midwives and nannies.

Early black settlers were blessed with strong church leaders such as: David George, Septimus Clarke, Boston King and Thomas Peters.

A historical highlight took place for Nova Scotia and blacks alike when in 1783, Rose Fortune of Annapolis Royal, became the first black person and the first policewoman in the province. Mrs. Fortune was also a successful businesswoman.

Another wave of eleven hundred black people left the American colonies, in 1783 for Nova Scotia. The first black Loyalist community was established in Birchtown. The other communities followed: Shelburne, Digby, Weymouth, Annapolis Royal, East Preston, Cherry Brook, Lake Loon, New Road (later renamed North Preston), Halifax, Lucasville and Tracadie.

Nova Scotian law interpreted the word 'slave' to mean: 'human property' for the sole ownership of white citizens. In short, a slave was not classified as a person with a soul worth saving. The truest definition of a slave: a non-person or a *'thing'*.

And do not think for a moment, that the religious leaders of the day, failed to engage in this debasing practice. Oddly enough, they were often the most sadistic of all slave masters. Their stern adherence to standards extended itself in the treatment of the poor and lowly slave. For instance, at minor infractions, one particular slave master, restricted his slave to iron shackles to be whipped.

As well, Nova Scotians were involved with the transaction of Polynesian Negroes and Africans, who were kidnapped and transported to slave ships in the southern states. They would be used for hard labour in the cotton fields, sugar plantations and the rum productions.

A particular slave owner in central Nova Scotia decided to teach his runaway slave a lesson. He pierced the slave's ear lobe and drew the end of the whip through it, which he had tied securely. The owner then rode his horse, thereby, dragging the unfortunate slave to his gruesome death… in that hellish state.

Ah, there seemed to be no place of comfort for the dispossessed black man, not even in the 'House of God'. In the early days, a good number of Negroes were baptized at St. Paul's Church, Halifax. However, upon entry, one Sunday, they were promptly ushered upstairs to sit in the church gallows.

Segregation is a psychological game. It is the next level up from slavery with its highly contradictory Christian principles. It seems that mainstream society had hoped that their foul treatment toward the black man and Native would mirror itself, to reflect a broken spirit.

A new immigration policy at Upper Canada (Ontario) was passed in 1739, thereby, restricting the entrance of American slaves into Canada.

The law legislated freedom to slaves of twenty-five years or more, but lacked total abolishment of slavery. This law cut like a dagger. What is freedom with restrictions?

In 1792, eleven hundred free black Loyalists left Nova Scotia and New Brunswick for emigration to Freetown, Sierra Leone, West Africa where they believed that their freedom would be better served.

Down in the West Indies, a group of Jamaican Maroons fought for their freedom in the Maroon War of 1795 to 1796. Back in 1655, when the British conquered Jamaica from the Spanish, they gained a total of 1500 African slaves. The Spanish owners immediately relinquished control. These Maroons tenaciously held on to their freedom for an incredible 141 years. They hid in the mountains, thereby, defying their pursuers until 1796. However, in 1796, the Jamaican government decided to exile the Maroons to Nova Scotia.

It was around this time, that Governor Wentworth of Nova Scotia was concerned that a French attack on Halifax was eminent. In preparation, he arranged that the Jamaicans be responsible for rebuilding the 3rd fortification of Halifax Citadel. A marvellously star-shaped, hilled fortress located in the midst of the city. The Maroons were skilled labourers. The stonemasons constructed the fort while the blacksmiths worked on the wrought iron fences of the cities' government buildings.

As well, Maroons were inducted into the militia such were: Officers Alexander Ochterloney and William Dawes Quarrel, Esq.

In fact, Dartmouth has two streets which reflect their namesake. Although, the name Quarrel was later changed to Queen Street.

However, most Maroons, along with several black Loyalist such as Boston King, desired to live in a more amicable and conducive environment. Hence on October 1, 1800, the group immigrated to Freetown, Sierra Leone, West Africa. Where Boston King left to pursue a career as a teacher and preacher.

In the 1800's, the City of Halifax operated a POW camp on the Melville Island Prison, near the head of the Northwest Arm. Captured seamen were detained there during the wars between Great Britain, France and the United States. In the American War of 1812–1814, the conflict raged against the British, who again, rallied the support of slaves in exchange for their freedom.

At this time, approximately 2000 blacks Refugees arrived in Nova Scotia and New Brunswick from Delaware and Chesapeake Bay via Bermuda. Nevertheless, the government was not pleased with their arrival and, in May of 1815, these Refugees were quarantined and vaccinated in the prison quarters on Melville Island.

Black Refugees initially, settled in Westphal (Dartmouth), but the Governor sent them to the backwoods. They settled anew in New Road, much later renamed North Preston; the last and most isolated of the Preston area communities. The following is an excerpt of an interview with eighty-year old Mrs. Beatrice (Johnson) Jackson, who was born in North Preston. Her mother, Mrs. Annie V (Beals) Johnson, was the best friend of Mom Suse.

> "If the truth be told, when we first arrived here, we began to settle on unclaimed land in Westphal. Soon after that, the government relocated us to the backwoods of (New Road) later called North Preston. Actually, we blacks were not the first people to settle in Westphal. A small group of [Mi'kmaq] Indians had settled there before us. The white community sent them packing into the woods. When we blacks arrived in North Preston, we were warmly greeted by the Indians. There we lived, side by side, alongside Long Lake. Most of the men took up logging and

trapping while the women, children and men went to town (Dartmouth and Halifax) to market their wares."[5]

Richard Preston escaped from the slave state of Virginia around 1816. It was Providence that he was able to locate his mother in East Preston, Nova Scotia. Apparently, she had identified him by a scar on his face. There is a great assumption that Richard changed his surname to Preston in order to divert his path from possible American slave trackers. Incidentally, the name Preston is also a location in Britain. Many of our provincial locations are named after areas in the British Isles, and other European localities.

The mechanics of slavery with its public slave auctions and private slave sales kept white families intact and increased with goods. To the black family all of this came with a price of emotional and financial bankruptcy... a serious erosion of dignity. Under these methods, it was not uncommon for children, infants and even newborns to be left as orphans. The fear of separation was real. It could come at any time, night or day. And most times... it did. Powerless, the black man could not protect his own family. He knew the highest degree of shame.

A few years later, Richard Preston was sent to school in England where upon completion, he was ordained as a Baptist Minister. After his return to Nova Scotia, he was responsible for establishing Halifax's first segregated black church in 1832. It was named, Cornwallis Street United Baptist Church. However, the original name given was the African United Baptist Church; a name the authorities would not accept.

Since 1843, Preston was a key contributor in the formation of the African United Baptist Association (AUBA). As time progressed, there would be more than 11 provincial African United Baptist Churches.

The blacks of Shelburne County were the descendants of the black Loyalists. They established Bethel African Methodist Episcopal Church. In time, the blacks were given no alternative, but to establish their own churches.

Mom Suse: Matriarch of the Preston area Black Communities

In the beginning, the white man brought Christianity to the Mi'kmaq and the black slave. Centuries later, the white man introduced segregation to the Mi'kmaq and black man. Yet, from the beginning to the end, it was the teacher who had refused to uphold the principles that he had so dearly professed to believe in.

For centuries in North America, the conscious and subconscious affects of slavery and segregation have had a negative impact on the First Nations, the black man, and the white man. Future societies desiring to desegregate the mindset of its citizens will have a difficult task in fostering cultural interaction and thus, to dispel countless years of engrained fear and ignorance. However, each successive generation, will reap a greater harvest than the proceeding one.

The bulk of runaway American slaves sought refuge in Canada. They clung to the hope of freedom. A hope that chains could not bind. From the first half of the 1800's, thousands upon thousands of runaway slaves escaped to the North via the 'Underground Railroad'.

This was not an actual railroad service above or underground. It was a secret connecting route system for escaped slaves. The escapees would travel, primarily, under cover-of-night by any means necessary from the Southern slave states to the Northern free states with the assistance of white and black Abolitionists alike. Their destination was Canada, the 'Land of Freedom' or the 'North Star'.

However, in 1800, a group of 95 discontented refugees left Nova Scotia for the tropical island of Trinidad. The grass was not always greener on the other side of the American border.

The Mi'kmaq band of St. Georges Bay, in Newfoundland, built a beautiful schooner in 1822. This was actually about 100 years prior the building of the *Bluenose,* the famous Nova Scotia schooner. The image of the *Bluenose* would be imprinted on the Canadian dime in 1921.

The birth of William E. Hall (1826-1904) in Horton, Hants County is well worth noting. In 1857, Hall received the Victoria Cross presented to him by Queen Victoria, herself, for participation in the Battle of Lucknow.

Hall was awarded the highest military honour in the British Commonwealth for valour, as a black seaman and gunner. In memoriam, his name is affixed to a Halifax branch of the Royal Canadian Legion.

In 1825, the Dartmouth Ferry service offered Mi'kmaq and black people a reduced passenger rate of a half penny (British currency). The regular passenger rate was four pence. This reduction in fare was accompanied by the prohibited use of the ladies cabin and the Upper Deck. Hence, the group was segregated strictly to the Main Deck. In 1906, this policy was lifted.

In 1834, the founding of the Nova Scotia Philanthropists Society established itself to acknowledge the plight of the Mi'kmaq and black man.

A few years earlier in 1832, a strain of Scarlet Fever afflicted Nova Scotians. It was a highly contagious viral disease. When left untreated, the patient succumbed to kidney ailments, rheumatic fever or death. At the eleventh hour, the Nova Scotia Philanthropists Society and the government provided medicine and food supplies. Again, in 1836, the disease repeated its reign of terror. Much to the chagrin of the families previously affected. It is believed that the government failed to act accordingly, after the first outbreak.

In terms of transportation services, Halifax continued to progress. In 1840, Samuel Cunard developed a steamship line to transport the Royal Mail between Britain and its' North American colonies.

The giant of Cape Breton, Angus McAskill (1825-1863), was born in Scotland, but lived and died in Cape Breton. McAskill grew to an astounding height of 8 ft. and weighted in at 400 lbs. It is strange but true, he was a real spectacle of the times.

Another famous Nova Scotian was Alexander Graham Bell (1844-1922). He was the inventor of the telephone. Although, Bell's significant contribution to aviation is not as well known. Later in life, he became a devoted educator of the Deaf.

In his memory, the Alexander Graham Bell National Historic Site of Canada was constructed in the Village of Baddeck, Cape Breton.

The Canadian population increased to over three million between 1815 and 1850. This was primarily due a great swell of immigrants from the British Isles. In Ireland, a large number fled from the fatal Potato Crop Famine of 1845 to 1847. However, they also struggled to live in Canada. Others fled from unjust labour conditions in the cotton factories and coalmines in England and Scotland. Unfortunately, where adults and children alike were employed. Some of these distraught, poverty-stricken labourers incited riots, and were responsible for the destruction of property. For this cause, several workers were unjustly sentenced to hanging or deportation to Australia.

Back in Nova Scotia, the relocation of the Mi'kmaq onto reservations placed on them an added stigma. As well, in 1851, the Canadian government created a new term, "Indian Status". This was instituted to cause a greater fracturing amongst Aboriginals.

The criteria devised to claim Indian Status, rested solely through the male lineage. Therefore, a Native woman who married a non-Native, along with any of their children, lost their claim for Indian Status. This policy would not be rescinded until 1985, when a total of 8,000 Mi'kmaq would re-instate their claims.

Political events stemming from the American Civil War (1861-1865), led Canada to seek political self-protection from Britain. This war seriously divided America. The Confederates in the South with their slave states wanted no interference into their illustrious lifestyle.

The Union, in the Northern free states bitterly opposed slavery. The Confederates and specifically, the British, profited greatly from slavery. In the end, the war ended badly for the South. Their loss of the war signalled the end of slavery. Hence, the Emancipation Proclamation was signed on January 1st, 1865, thereby, abolishing slavery in the United States of America.

Since Halifax was initially established as the hub of British operations, the province prospered by providing services to the British military. Times were especially fruitful during colonial resistance. Thus, the Civil War brought a great upsurge in commercial activity to the province, where the British sentiment was at its zenith.

However, Britain felt the financial strain of war, coupled with the burden of maintaining its Canadian colonies. This was a burden waiting to be lifted, and Canada was ready to be loosed from the 'apron strings' of Britain. Therefore, on July 1,1867, Confederation

Vivian Willis

was achieved in Charlottetown, Prince Edward Island. Canada had become a new Dominion.

CHAPTER 3

After the War of 1812, when the blacks settled in New Road (later renamed North Preston) they were warmly greeted by a band of Mi'kmaq Indians. The Mi'kmaq were also chased into these woods before them. Some blacks and Mi'kmaq found work in the coalmines, but the working conditions were deplorable. Over a period of time, several cave-ins occurred causing the men to search for work elsewhere. Unfortunately, discrimination made this pursuit a daily struggle. A few turned to farming but, the land was not the most fertile, many supplemented this business with farm animals.

The authorities left our people in the backwoods with very few provisions. However, the following spring they (the authorities) returned 'up home' with empty carts. These carts were to hold our dead. In the exact words of our ancestor's, "we were not expected to last the winter". But, thanks be to God, who through our prayer of sustenance, provided for us in the form of the Indians.

It is a known fact that we would *not* have survived, without their continual assistance. Hence, by 1820, the population of the Preston communities totalled 958 people. ***We owe a special gratitude to our family, the Mi'kmaw.***

Nova Scotia's black communities flourished in the 1800's and Africville, was no exception. This community was sheltered in haven of the Bedford Basin. Their land originally stretched out way beyond Yonge Street and the Halifax Commons.

Africville had its success stories in George Dixon (1870-1909), who became a hero in the boxing ring. He was the first fighter to win three World Boxing titles. Dixon was known as 'Little Chocolate'. In respect and memory of his achievements, Halifax constructed, the George Dixon Recreation Centre. The self-sufficiency of the residents of Africville was evident in 1883, when they managed, funded and operated their own community school.

Halifax's black community also has a hero in James Robinson Johnston (1876-1915). In 1898, this outstanding academic would be the first black Nova Scotian to break the colour barrier and graduate with a Law Degree from Dalhousie University. Johnston practiced Law in 1901, until he was shot down at the tender age of thirty-nine. The legacy of 'Lawyer Johnston' will *never*, ever be forgotten.

In 1881, the segregated school system in Halifax created several problems causing blacks to protest. The situation would, invariably grow worse before positive changes would come.

Another young boxer emerged from the black community. He was Sam Langford (1884-1965) of Weymouth, Digby County. Langford had been one of the greatest fighters in the history of boxing. In his memory, the Sam Langford Community Centre was built in Weymouth Falls.

From 1890 to 1912, a total of 1,736 West Indian workers arrived in Nova Scotia. They settled in the counties of Pictou, Antigonish, Guysborough, and on the island of Cape Breton. There, they laboured in the numerous coalmines that dotted the area.

The black presence had become a viable force in the Cape Breton. Their four black communities: Whitney Pier in Sydney, Sterling in Glace Bay, the third in North Sydney and a fourth in New Waterford.

Under the Indian Act of 1876, the government instituted policies to further quench the existing autonomy of our First Nations. Nonetheless, in 1901, the Mi'kmaq flag was proudly flown in Halifax, Nova Scotia.

Chapter 4

Mom Suse's great grandparents came to Nova Scotia from America along with other black refugees at the onset of the War of 1812, against the British. Many settled in the Preston area (East Preston, Cherry Brook and Lake Loon).

The beginnings of the New Road community. The Indians created a well-worn path north of the Preston area. Sometime after the mid-1800, it was built as a new road; hence, the original name of, 'New Road'. This very long upward-winding road led to a small, but growing community' deep in the backwoods. As well, the Indians had made a path from East Preston to New Road through a back road. This back road would later border on the edge of Mom Suse's property to connect with the main road.

Mom Suse's maternal grandmother, Annie Turner lived in Cherry Brook and after marrying Daniel Cain, she moved to New Road. She was Métis (Mi'kmaq and Irish). This was at a time when Nova Scotian society did not approve of inter-racial marriages with Caucasians.

During the 1840's Annie Turner worked on the farm that supported the 'Coloured Children's Orphanage'. As farmers before her, Annie's ancestors had worked the land for many years. The large Orphanage consisted of a two-room Primary School with barns and chicken houses.

This is where Annie met her future husband, Daniel Cain. He was an African, an Ethiopian Jew, now living in New Road. Daniel was employed as a farm hand at the Orphanage. He made his way to freedom in Canada via the "Underground Railroad". He was also a recent ex-slave from a plantation in Alabama.

The courtship between Annie Turner and Daniel Cain was pure destiny. He was intrigued with her from the very start. Her determination to succeed, regardless of the obstacles, endeared her to him. At the beginning, he was intent to simply watch and admire how she took everything in stride. But after awhile, he realized that he would have to find the courage to talk to her and find out how she felt about him.

The next day, the opportunity arose when she was changing the bed linens. As Daniel approached her, he decided, it was' now or never'.

"Hello Annie," said Daniel, after he introduced himself. "I sure am glad to be working on this here Orphanage farm, or we'd never have met."

"Why, thank you," responded Annie, in delight.

"It sure is hard work, but its work, in the end," said Daniel.

"Yes, that's the way I feel too! Me and my family, we work hard to take care of one another," stated Annie.

"I know what you mean," said Daniel kindly. "I left all my family back home in Alabama – that's where I came from ya' know. I sure do feel bad that they couldn't make it up here, like me."

"You must have had it pretty bad Daniel," said Annie, in a caring voice. She instinctively gave him a friendly hug to let him know that she sympathized with his sorrow.

"It's just not fair! People working so-o hard and still treated… much worse than animals," recalled a clearly frustrated Daniel.

"That's all behind you now Daniel. I'm sure you can make a good life for yourself, now that you are a free man up here in Nova Scotia," Annie assured him.

"Hopefully, that is what I am counting on," said Daniel. "I think this country's a good place to live. At least, I am free here and I'm no stranger to hard work."

"That is why I like you," Annie said, shyly. "I admire a man who's not afraid to work hard."

"You're a hard worker yourself and a mighty pretty one at that!" Daniel commented.

Annie blushed past her response, "Why thank you Daniel, that's very nice of you to say so."

"I only say what I mean. You *are* the finest lady I've met - a genuinely nice human being, and one of the kindest," revealed Daniel.

Annie sincerely repaid the compliment.

"And I'll always remember your kind words. Would... would, would you like to come to dinner one night and meet my family?" Annie offered.

"I'd be delighted," said Daniel gratefully, but looking a little surprised.

"How, how about tomorrow night?" Annie asked quickly, before she lost her nerve.

"Tomorrow, oh tomorrow's just fine Annie, just fine," replied Daniel, sounding happier than he had been in months.

"I'm glad that you accepted Daniel, I wanted to ask you before but..."

Daniel was so excited with the offer that he interrupted her train of thought.

"I'm sure glad you did. I'm looking forward to meeting your family. They sound like good people from what you've told me," stated Daniel.

"I know they would be honoured to meet you. I've told them so much about you already," said Annie. Now it was Daniel's turn to blush.

At the end of the day they bid each other farewell. Yet, instead of separating, they lingered in the front hall of the orphanage.

"I guess our work day is finished, but at least, its money and people gotta eat," Daniel said, unwilling to let the moment go.

That's the way I look at it too!" Annie commented, enthusiastically.

"I can't stand the ones who are always complaining and don't want to help themselves. They always annoy me," added Daniel.

"Those kinds of people wouldn't have a chance where I came from. Why, when anything like that was tried on the plantation, the Overseer would beat us, and often just for sport. He'd torture us, 'til we either kept working or died. It was **Hell**, but believe it or not, God *was* in the midst. How else could we have survived that demon called, 'slavery'?" questioned Daniel.

"Um, I sure am glad you made you it up here," said Annie. "Nova Scotia needs more men like you, who aren't afraid of hard work. Now, don't go forgetting about dinner tomorrow night," Annie emphasized.

"How could I forget an invitation like that, from such a lovely lady as yourself," said Daniel.

"I'll say goodnight, then," said Annie, obviously overjoyed at the attention she was receiving.

"Goodnight, Annie," Daniel offered his hand. Annie shyly averted his gaze as she gripped his hand. They parted, reluctantly.

For Annie and Daniel, the next day went by, all too slowly. They were looking forward to dinner that night. Finally, after what seemed an eternity, the workday at the Orphanage came to a close.

Since Daniel had arrived on the East Coast, this was to be the first time that he would be invited to dinner and, with the woman he admired. Daniel was ecstatic! This was to be a truly special occasion.

"I'm glad the day's work is finally over," said Daniel, unable to hide the weariness in his voice.

"Me too!" Annie added, while nodding in agreement.

"I'm looking forward to you coming home for dinner tonight," said Annie.

"I have been thinking of it all day. Seems like time just crawled along. Oh, I forgot to ask you, what time do you want me over?" Daniel asked.

"Oh, about seven o'clock," answered Annie, remembering to give him the directions. "I'm going home to clean up, but you'll be there on time, won't you Daniel?" Asked Annie, with concern.

"You can count on it!" He exclaimed.

"My family is real anxious to meet you," revealed Annie.

"See you at seven!" said Daniel, eagerly.

Daniel wasted no time preparing for his date. With one eye on the time, he washed up and dressed in his Sunday best. The trip on horseback was short and without incident. He tethered his horse in front of the Turner's house. As he looked ahead, he saw Annie waiting for him on the front porch.

"I saw you dismount from your horse," said Annie. "Man, you're right on time."

Daniel spoke quietly. "The last thing I wanted to do was to show up late. Ever since you invited me, I could think of nothing else."

Outside of the work environment, he suddenly felt ill at ease, but Annie's cheerful tone, and animated mannerism quickly dispelled his nervousness.

"I'm only sorry I didn't invite you earlier." Annie admitted.

Daniel suppressed a chuckle and replied, "That's okay Annie. I've been really busy on the farm. I still have a lot to do before the weather changes. Shall we go in Annie?" he asked. She quietly led the way.

Annie's parents, two sisters and three brothers were in the parlour waiting anxiously to meet her beau. Annie's father, Sam Turner stepped forward to meet the young man. His first impression was favourable. Daniel was clean-cut, polite and had a firm handshake.

"Hello Daniel. My name is Sam Turner. We've heard a lot about you, and it's nice to finally meet you in person," said Mr. Turner.

"I've been looking forward to it sir," said Daniel.

"Please call me Sam. From what I've heard, you're working hard to make something of yourself. Any person who thinks the way I do, should be on a first-name basis."

"Thanks Sam. I appreciate that," replied Daniel, gratefully.

"I've always believed in hard work, myself," said Sam, as he motioned for Daniel to be seated.

"In fact, I build this house myself. Anyway, let me introduce you to the rest of the family."

This here, is my beautiful wife Sara, my sons Jake, Tom and Amos. Over here are my daughters, Rebecca and Ruth."

"I'm very happy to meet all of you. I've heard so much about this family," responded Daniel.

Sara spoke for the first time. "Annie has told us a lot of nice things about you. It's good to know that they're all true. Well, it is time for dinner now! Shall we sit down and eat?"

Everyone went into the kitchen and sat around at the harvest-style table. "We are having rabbit stew, Daniel," Sara said, as she ladled a generous portion into a bowl.

"I hope you like it," added Sara.

"It smells great. I sure am hungry, " said Daniel, still trying to contain his happiness.

"So am I," agreed Sam. "And my wife is an excellent cook."

They all enjoyed the meal, but none as much as Daniel. When it was over, everybody retired to the parlour with a cup of tea.

Since I came to Nova Scotia, that was the best dinner I've had," said Daniel, looking to Sara in appreciation.

"Mrs. Turner, you really are a good cook."

Sara chuckled, "If it wasn't for Sam's traps, we wouldn't have had this stew for dinner. And I couldn't have done it without my daughter's help. She's a far better cook than I am."

"Oh Mom, don't say that. I'll never be able to cook meals like you," said Annie.

Daniel and Annie shared the moment…. he gave her a wink and an approving smile.

In order to impress her guest, Sara Turner had spent all day slaving over a hot stove. She was pleased with her daughter's compliment. Although she knew her family was impressed with her meals, it never hurt when one of them mentioned it.

As the rest of the family tended to the dishes, and kitchen clean up, Annie and Daniel went for an evening stroll along the field. The length and breadth of the moonlight illuminated their path.

"Look!" Annie said, pointing to the sky. "There's a full moon out tonight."

Daniel paused long enough to face his gorgeous date. He circled his arms around her small waist and tenderly pulled her closer. Under the romantic moonlight, they shared a tender kiss.

"You really are the most beautiful woman in the world. If, I didn't know any better, I'd swear that I'd died and gone to heaven," said Daniel, as he affectionately stroked her cheek. They shared another kiss before Annie pulled away.

"Well, I really should… should be getting back," said Annie, breathlessly. I don't think my parents will be happy, if I stay out late."

"That's all right," said Daniel, "I have to get up early for work, anyway."

"Me too!" Annie added.

"Allow me to walk you to the front door," said Daniel. Instinctly, they reached for one another's hand and lingered on the front porch; not ready to disturb the magic of the moment.

Once more, they kissed before Annie paused and reluctantly opened the door.

Daniel thanked Sam and Sara for having him over, then bent down and whispered into Annie's ear.

"You made this evening really beautiful for me. I feel like I am walking on air. I didn't dare dream that it would turn out so well."

There were many more dinners and romantic walks in the nearby fields, before Daniel admitted to himself that he had fallen head over heels in love.

The more he saw Annie, the more he realized that no other woman could possibly match his love for her. Finally, he could wait no longer.

After enjoying several home cooked meals, Daniel waited nervously until Annie suggested a stroll in the fields. This was the moment he was waiting for, even though he feared that she would turn him down. Nonetheless, he plunged ahead. Daniel was ready to propose to his beloved Annie, here and now.

"Annie," said Daniel, as he held his hands in hers and gazed in her bright green eyes.

"You are the only woman I want to spend my life with." He paused and tried to control his racing heartbeat. He had gone too far, to turn back now?

"Would... would you do me the honour of being my wife?" There was a moment of silence, but to Daniel it seemed like an eternity.

When a grin slowly formed on Annie's face, Daniel's heart leaped for joy.

"You're the only man I'll ever love," said Annie, her voice choking with emotion.

"I'll consider myself the luckiest girl on earth, if I were your wife, Daniel. Of course, I'll marry you!" Exclaimed an elated Annie.

Daniel held Annie's waist and twirled her around before warming her heart with his strong embrace. Perhaps, time stood still in the semi-darkness, because the only sounds they could hear were the beating of their hearts.

"I was so afraid you were going to turn me down," exclaimed Daniel, unable to believe his ears. "You… you did say 'yes', didn't you?"

"I sure did my handsome husband-to-be." Annie stretched her body to stand tippy-toe. She placed her arms around his shoulders to whisper in his ear.

"Of course my parents will have to agree. But I don't think that will be a problem. They like you, almost as much as I do," admitted Annie.

"That's a relief," said Daniel. He chuckled as he remembered practicing the question in front of his bedroom mirror.

"I sure hope you're right about your parents. I don't want anything to ruin our sweet love. I want to share the rest of my life with you," he added.

Annie and Daniel embraced once again before they returned to the farmhouse. The moment of truth! Now he was about to ask her father for her hand in marriage. As they approached the front door, Daniel hesitated.

Once again, doubt filled his mind. If her parents didn't agree to the nuptials, Daniel wouldn't know what to do. Annie's smile encouraged his soul. She led him to the front door. "Don't worry about my parents," she assured him.

Sara Turner greeted them at the door and invited them into the parlour. Daniel coughed and cleared his throat, an obvious sign of trepidation. "Mr. Turner," he said, finally breaking the uneasy silence.

"No need to be so formal, remember that it's 'Sam' to you. Ask away son," said Sam smiling as if he knew what to expect.

"Sir, I want to ask your permission to marry your daughter, Annie." Both Sara and Sam broke into big grins. Sam stood up to shake the hand of his future son-in-law.

"This is what my wife and I have been waiting for. Welcome to the family, Daniel!" Mr. Turner exclaimed.

The next workday, Daniel and Annie were filled with an indescribable joy. It left them hard pressed to concentrate on their work. As Annie washed up the dinner dishes she caught a glimpse of her sweet love, through the kitchen window. He was working out in the fields.

"My, oh my, God sure is good to me," whispered Annie. At the same moment, a blue jay quietly perched itself on the outside window's ledge. The bird proudly displayed its pointed crown.

Annie was an avid bird watcher and awed by this revelation of God's love. She had to get a closer glimpse of her little 'visitor'.

Annie walked quickly to the door. As quiet as possible, she opened the screen door. But the slightest squeak of the rusty hinges startled the little creature. To Annie's chagrin, her visitor flew overhead as if, to bid her 'farewell'. She was slightly dejected until she stepped outside and felt the rays of the midday sun. It invited her to accept its warmth.

There she stood gazing toward the woods where the blue jay had flown. Annie was totally unaware that the sun's subtle intensity had caused Daniel to remove his shirt. She looked over yonder once more and smiled. As he

toiled, sweat beads shone on his brow. Annie decided to surprise him with a tall glass of ice-cold lemonade. While she carried the drink to him, the nearness of his manly scent filled her with laughter. Just for fun, Daniel pretended not to notice, but her fragrance had awakened his senses. My, it was sweet and light, just like her laughter. Now, his back was facing her. Wait a minute! Something awful had caught her vision.

Annie made an abrupt stop! Her enlarged eyes met a horrific sight. After a few deep breaths she inched toward Daniel who had turned slightly sideways. She looked so stunned that he was worried she might faint; he said a quick prayer.

Annie could do nothing but stare at his hideously scarred back. She shook her head back and forth, in disbelief. The silence lingered except for the four ice cubes that rattled in the glass. They struggled in their transparent prison, as if, for territorial rights.

Mechanically, Annie reached out to give him the cold beverage. Graciously, he nodded in acceptance. Daniel drank it in one gulp, while keeping an eye on her. It wasn't the first time she had come face to face with the scars of slavery. It's just that, it was always *so* overwhelming.

This time it would 'cut' much closer. These scars also belonged to her. Annie could not imagine what agonies he had suffered. She really didn't want to know. Her eyes had filled with tears. The first tear escaped to the warmth of her cheek. It was soon followed by the release of the others. Daniel bent down to set his glass on the shirt. Upon rising he leaned over to kiss away her tears. He held her in a loving embrace, and whispered with all the compassion he could muster.

"It's O.K. Annie, I… I have never seen what my back looks like. It must be awful bad! The, the physical agony is gone, now." Daniel paused to collect his thoughts.

"Ya' know Annie, I still have nightmares sometimes… someday they will stop. Honey, the scars will *never* disappear. But, at least now… the physical torture is over," added Daniel.

It was Daniel who needed to be comforted. Annie pulled out a tissue from her apron pocket. She wiped her eyes, stuffed the tissue back and re-positioning her arms around his strong form. Her hands moved strangely over the imperfect ridges of keloid skin. She *would* find a way to get used to this. It seemed as if the scars mapped out his entire back. In order to, maintain her composure, Annie let out a couple of heavy sighs.

"Baby," she said, "I do believe, that we can soar like eagles over the trials of life." It is in times like these that the soul is embraced with the tranquility of God.

Chapter 5

My grandparents, Annie and Daniel Cain, lived in New Road. But my parents, Adeline and John Bundy were from Cherry Brook. At the turn of the century, in 1904, I, Susannah Bundy married Demus Smith of New Road. As newlyweds, we had not yet known how to read or write. So we marked an, 'X' on the signature line of our marriage certificate. We were positive thinkers, and in time, Demus and I taught ourselves how to read and write quite well.

It is interesting to note that no sooner had we 'jumped the broom', that I found myself, well... 'in the family way'. We lived with my parents until Demus built our homestead. It was to be complete with a two-story farmhouse, a stable, a barn, a chicken house, a pig house, a doghouse, and of course, an outhouse. Our acreage was large. Upon entering New Road, I would travel up the hill to view our property on the right.

The hilltop view of Long Lake was just grand. We lived in harmony with the Indians and inter-married in the backwoods of New Road. Dating back from the late 1800's, Mi'kmaq and black folk sold our wares regularly in town. Unfortunately, a time came when the government herded all full-blooded Indians to a 'reservation of segregation' in Shubenacadie. We lost our husbands, wives, and wives with children, including grandparents, etc.

Only God understood our duel sufferings. Since then, our community has continually mourned the loss of our native heritage.

As well, we also traded with the Mi'kmaq band from Turtle's Cove, Dartmouth. For those of us going to market, the one-way trek into town was a about a nine and a half mile walk from New Road.

Vivian Willis

We arose before dawn in preparation to catch the Dartmouth ferry to Halifax. Men, women and children alike, lugged our produce and wares in all types of weather.

However, I was fortunate enough to own a horse and buggy that I harnessed for the trip. In preparation, to keep us cozy in the buggy, we heated a large stone in the oven as our 'warming stone'. This was then wrapped and placed under our feet for the long trip ahead. We were warmed for a long time.

The Dartmouth Ferry Terminal had Approaches that serviced the horses, oxen with wagons, horse and buggies, including automobiles. These were all transported on the ferries' Lower Deck. Blacks and Mi'kmaq were relegated to the Main Deck for a reduced fare minus the use of washroom facilities while the Upper Deck was reserved for the white folks.

Other than the ferry, the only other route into Halifax, was the longer route by way of the Dartmouth side of the Bedford Basin and around to Halifax.

Along with many women from our community, we travelled daily to sell our baked goods, preserves, fresh produce, and varieties of fresh berries, mayflowers and piles of kindling wood. By the way, Demus rose early to chop the kindling that I sold.

The craftspeople in our midst were weavers of baskets, brooms and hats, to name a few. Also, our friends and family the Mi'kmaq, made gorgeous items with porcupine quills, birch bark, beading, woodwork and more. As well, many of us painstakingly created, various seasonal crafts such as highly attractive Christmas wreaths.

I also worked as a sales clerk and cleaner at Mr. Mitchell's Drug store in Halifax. The pastry sold in his store, was my home baking.

Several of our community women found work as domestic help in homes or as nannies. Others worked in stores or institutions. And don't ask how hard we worked. For most of our folk, domestic work was a 'killer'. Some employers could ***never*** be pleased. Only the Good Lord knows how ***hard*** we worked.

Finally our homestead was completed. Our families pitched in, to help with the move. My father, John Bundy, was the self-appointed team supervisor. He seemed content to pretend to 'holler' directions at everyone.

"Okay Henry, you and James can move that couch into the parlour, and be careful! I don't think Suse will appreciate any rips in the upholstery," commented Dad. Henry laughed in his good-natured way.

"Sure thing Pops. I won't want to do anything like that, 'specially when Demus just got finished paying it off," said Henry.

My brother, Gerald, stuck his head up from behind a box and inhaled the aroma of freshly baked brownies and shortbread cookies.

"Suse, I'd know the smell of your brownies, a mile away," said Gerald.

I laughed and replied, "Just you wait, Gerald Bundy. If you want some of *my* baking, you're gonna have to do a lot more work than what you've done, so far."

"Okay, Suse, you win! Now I'll work twice as hard," responded Gerald.

Demus' brothers, Dan and Fleming tried to move a huge oak dresser from the buggy to the front porch. Dan struggled with the greatest weight of the furniture.

"You know Fleming," wheezed Dan, "I'd swear this dresser was nailed to the ground… it's just so heavy." Fleming grunted as sweat glistened on his forehead.

"You got that right brotha' and that ain't no word of a lie," said Fleming. They both laughed so hard; they had to ease the dresser down on the porch.

"If we think this is bad, we sure wouldn't want to be lugging any of that 18th century Chippendale furniture. You know, the kind from England. They say it weights a ton… and it's some expensive," Fleming remarked.

"Uh mm, well the price of furniture here in Nova Scotia, is enough to make a poor man cry! I heard that at a store over in Halifax, they're charging $9.25 for an enamelled brass bed. Thank God that a lot of this here stuff's been donated," said Dan, proudly.

John watched the Smith boys at work, and called out to them. "You two are working up such a sweat, after you get inside why don't you try and sneak a cookie or two from Suse? Looks like you two need an energy boost!" Dad commented.

"That's fine to say Dad, but don't try to get past Suse 'cause that lady has eyes in the back of her head," replied Fleming, trying to ignore the strain on his muscles.

Dad grinned and shot right back. "Oh I think Suse could be sweet talked into handing over a couple of cookies to such hard working men."

Demus took a break from unloading the buggy. As he walked toward the house, he past by the porch and offered his brothers a hand. Demus was glad that they declined his offer. If the truth be told, he needed a break… and was glad for it. Once inside, he entered the parlour where tried to find the most available seat amidst a bunch of boxes. He sat on the corner of the red

velvet antique loveseat. He attempted to relax by shifted himself to a more comfortable position.

Demus spied Dad walking past the stairwell door and hoped that he too, was ready for a break.

"You know, Mr. Bundy, the other day I heard tell that Alaska is now in the hands of the Americans," recalled Demus.

"Oh, and why is that?" Dad asked, as he entered the parlour and squeezed in beside his son-in-law.

"On account of the folks in England. It turned out that they didn't back up Canada on the deal," answered Demus.

"Oh, it figures, you can't trust anyone, nowadays," said Dad.

"Say, I hear that the Dominion Coal workers got a 5¢ pay increase, up from 20¢ per hour. The night shift workers' raise was up from 30¢," Demus reported.

"That should help some with the cost of living," said Dad.

"It's a crying shame! In order to clothe a family today, a man would have to have a fortune. A little girl's dress sells for $1.49, and a lady's coat about $5.00. Well, a pair of ladies gloves can run you at 15¢. Why even at a men's store in town, a sweater for both boys and men, sells for $2.50. And get this! It costs a whole $5.00 to register an automobile but it's a one-time fee – that's the good thing about it," said Demus, a bit long-winded.

"Well we won't have to worry about that for awhile yet," commented Dad, as he tried to get a word in.

Mom Suse: Matriarch of the Preston area Black Communities

At times Demus could be so loquacious. Dad stood up and gave a little stretch. He spoke in an authoritative voice, "Oh, I do believe it's time to get back to supervising. I don't like to see men lazin' around, you know!"

With all of the help provided, the move was completed by the end of the day. Our two-storey homestead was lavishly furnished. Generally speaking, this was not the norm. In our community, many lived in modest homes. But others lived in shacks until they could afford to upgrade.

Thankfully, my employers and customers donated many of the furniture items. Our house was set a little ways from the road. The front porch was a good size where company could relax on a hot summer's day. To the right of the front door there was a coat closet, a mirrored hat rack and an umbrella stand. The wide hallway stretched from the front door, past the parlour, the door to the stairwell leading upstairs and, to the dining room.

The end of the hallway welcomed you into the large kitchen. The flooring in the kitchen and hallway was made of oilcloth. Hardwood covered the other floors on both levels of the house. A multitude of rugs, not only protected, but also tastefully decorated the floors. From the font door entrance, the left side of the kitchen was visible.

To the left of the hallway a little past the parlour was the stairwell door. It led upstairs to the four large bedrooms. Each bedroom had a kerosene oil lamp set on an oak table that stood beside the bed. The head of the bed was placed at the far right back corner. The large mirrored dresser was placed along the left wall. The smaller oak table for the enamelled pitcher and basin was set at the left entrance. The attic stored a myriad of furniture and miscellaneous stuff.

On the main level next to the coatroom was the parlour with its lavish display of antique furniture. The loveseat was placed at the left entrance of the parlour. Beside the loveseat was a couch decorated with a mahogany border complete with short end tables and an oval mahogany coffee table. On the right wall of the parlour stood Demus' prized possession, his organ. The rocking chair sat in between the organ and the oil lamp table. At the top right-hand corner was a shelved-table where the Gramophone was placed. It had replaced the old tin-cylinder Phonograph, since 1887, by reproducing a much greater sound. Our wood stove was situated at the back wall. It also used coal. The stove kept the front rooms on both levels nice and warm. Further down the long hallway was the dinning room with a large harvest-like mahogany table and chairs in the midst. The set included, of course, an armchair for Demus.

The matching mahogany china cabinet and hutch were centered against the back wall. A stately grandfather clock stood tall and regal, at the back left corner. The three-tier oak-serving cart was placed between the clock and the china cabinet. The right-hand corner housed the oak table for the oil lamp.

The kitchen was the last and largest room on the main floor. The left side of the kitchen was visible from the front entrance where one could see the shameless protruding pot-bellied stove and a portion of kitchen window.

The stove accepted both coal and wood, but it took up way too much room. I really couldn't wait for my husband to buy me a smaller stove. Although, I had to admit, it heated the back rooms on both levels, some good! There were two good-size sinks under the kitchen windows. The kitchen table and chairs stood in the midst of the floor. The set included, of course, Demus' armchair. The oil lamp was placed on the oak table at the upper right corner.

A large tub complete with an attached manual wringer was displayed against the right wall. The wooden-framed scrub board stood alone, in the tub. Beside it was a thick wooden-framed icebox insulated with a heavy tin interior. The bottom ice tray held large chunks of ice. Several men from New Road worked in the ice factory in Dartmouth. They were often given large broken ice pieces. Normally, the ice would have cost them 1¢ per pound.

The family's well was located outside the back door, not too far from the kitchen. A pantry was situated in the back room, to the right of the kitchen.

This is where I kept the food provisions and my pedal Singer Sewing machine. Demus constructed a built-in corner ironing board. He marvelled at the manner in which I pressed the clothes by heating the iron on the pot-bellied stove.

After the move was completed, our mother, Adeline, sister Lily and myself were busy in preparation for the families' first meal in the new house. The only person missing was my older sister, Lena, who had moved to Boston, some time ago. The dining table featured an enormous spread of food. I can smell it now! The men gathered in the parlour for a cup of tea and some down home conversation. Fleming intercepted John and gave him a soft poke in the ribs.

"What did I tell you? All that work, and no cookies or brownies in sight! There's no one around to sweet talk," said Fleming.

"Tell me about it," Dad joked. "I wanted some of those brownies myself," he added.

As the two chuckled, I appeared in the doorway and motioned everyone over to the dining room. "Dinner's ready!" I announced, gladly.

The tired and hungry movers didn't need any more coaxing. After washing their hands, they really enjoyed the cooking of the Bundy women. And they were a witness as to why Adeline and her daughters had a reputation in the community as great cooks. Moreover, if it had slipped anyone's mind, they would have only needed to inhale the succulent aroma that permeated the air.

When all had been seated, I called out, "Who'd like to say grace?"

"I think Demus should have the honour," Dad noted gravely, "seeing as how, he's the head of this house."

Everyone applauded in agreement. Demus lowered his head, cleared his throat and began the grace.

"Father God, thank you for the beautiful family and home that have placed before me. Bless the many hands that prepared this food," said Demus.

Then he turned his head to throw me a wink. Of course, I pretended not to sense his love and smiled shyly, without sharing his glance.

"And Lord Jesus," continued Demus, "thank you for the trials that come our way – they bring us closer to you. Bless us with your presence and love. And may this food be good for our bodies," concluded Demus.

After a slight pause, everyone chorused gratefully, "Amen!"

"That was real beautiful Demus," Adeline said.

"Thanks Mom Bundy. I meant every word of it," replied Demus.

"I've no doubt that you did," said Mom.

Then she turned to the hungry group and called out. "Go ahead, dip in 'cause it's time to eat!"

The conversation ebbed as the hands of hungry men and women passed around platters piled high with thick slabs of roast beef and ham along with steaming bowls of potatoes and vegetables. The initial pangs of hunger were soothed and the talk around the table centered on the succulent food.

"I've been working hard all day, and all I could think of was you girls cooking up a feast. And sure enough, you never disappoint us," said Demus, between mouthfuls of food.

"I'm so glad you're hungry Demus, because we slaved hard over that stove, **all** day. We even cooked with a new vegetable oil product. It's cheaper, and they say it's supposed to be healthier than butter or animal fat," I reported, as I smiled at my love. Demus reached over and tenderly squeezed my arm.

"I sure do appreciate the consideration over our health. Dear, I know that you slaved hard all day, and I you know how much I love your cooking," complimented Demus.

He chuckled, and added, "See what a great wife I have folks? Truly, I am a blest man."

For Demus and myself, our union was truly a unique affair. In fact, Demus had quietly quoted this old poem to me… as he often saw fit.

> "Conjugal life without love is a lamp without oil, a well without water and a sail without wind. There are no more serious or holier relations than lover, wife [mother]; or lover, husband, father."[6]

After finishing the housework in my new home, I relaxed with a steaming cup of cocoa and looked out of my kitchen window. I watched Demus put the finishing touches on the other buildings.

"I'm sure glad to see that the homestead will be completed in time for our first born. Now he'll have space to grow up. My, my, these winters sure are long and cold," I whispered, while patting my swollen tummy.

I continued to talk lovingly to my unborn child as if, expecting a response.

"He sure does think a lot of you baby. I hope you are a boy 'cause Demus could use some lot of help," I added.

I remained by the kitchen window completely still when I saw the chickadees and nuthatches chirping around the trees. They ate the bread, suet and seeds that I left for them each morning.

I obviously shared my grandmother's passion for birds. In fact, I was still at the window when a knock on the kitchen door gave me a startle.

"Whoa, Annie, how nice of you to drop over. Come on in, out of the biting cold while I fetch you a hot cup of cocoa," I said, being both surprised and happy at the same time.

"Annie laughed. "Why, how did you know what I wanted, Suse?"

"Well, I imagined that if my dearest and best friend, none other than, Annie V. Johnson, ventured out in the biting cold to see me then, at the least, she deserves a friendly smile… and a steaming cup of cocoa," I exclaimed.

"Suse, I only travelled up hill, from the Johnson Road. You know, that it's not that far," said Annie.

Annie was delighted at the offer and sat down at the kitchen table. As she sipped the cocoa, she carried a slight look of concern.

"How are you and the baby doing? "I'm sure you're anxiously awaiting his or her arrival," Annie asked.

"I'm doing just fine, considering it's my first baby," I replied.

Annie's laughter had put me at ease.

"Don't worry girl, you have nothing to worry about. I was worried before my firstborn, but I have two little ones now and they're both doing well. Right now, my older sister is giving me a little break by watching over little Violet and baby Gladys. Trust me. You have a loving husband in Demus, and girl, that's what's going to count in the long run," assured Annie.

I put her hand on my friend's shoulder. "Do you know something Annie, you always make me feel better about things, " I said.

"That reminds me... Suse, have you ever heard of Cato's song?" Annie asked.

"Hmm, no I can't say I have. What's the tune of it?" I questioned.

"Mama used to sing it to me when I was a little girl," said Annie.

"The song was sung by a plantation slave, who believed that a couple should study one another's character, instead of looking for present fulfillment before contemplating the conjugal union... if you know what I mean." Annie tilted her head slightly, and positioned her pretty dark eyes in a serious pose.

"Oh yes, Annie, I know exactly what you mean, do I ever!" I exclaimed, rather shyly.

Annie paused a bit, to collect her thoughts. Suse, it's written in slave talk and it goes like this:

> "Ef you seek true friend or lober
> Upward too de road you take –
> Hearts should neber travel downward
> Else dey mighty apt to break."[7]

"Hm, it's, it's real short, Annie. Where's the rest of the song?" I quizzed.

"Suse, you don't expect me to sing the whole thing, do ya'?" Annie asked.

"Oh, so you don't know the rest of the song, do you Annie? You *are* trying to get away with singing just a few lines," I protested, playfully.

"Suse, I ain't in no shape to sing the whole thing today," Annie replied rather defensively, but not harsh.

"My baby kept me up all night. You know, teething problems. And then, once I finally got her back to sleep. Well, my Willoughby said that he was feeling a little **cold**," said Annie, with another twinkle in her pretty dark eyes. Suse, I'm a little tired right now. Oh, you just wait 'til you have your baby – then you'll understand what I mean. After the babies come, the responsibilities increase," concluded Annie.

I tried to redeem myself.

"Oh I suppose, I suppose so Annie. Well... well you did do a good job, and the words are timeless."

"Um hm, Suse, don't you get the feeling that the worldly attitude of today is leading the youth astray?" Annie questioned.

"Girl, now tell the truth and shame the devil!" I responded, empathically and Annie shook her head in agreement.

"And he can stand to shamed," added Annie.

"Why just last night, Demus heard that over in England and America, it's a criminal offence to either speak or publish words that destroy the sanctity of our Heavenly Father. You know, blasphemy!" I exclaimed.

"Ah! The respect of our Lord and Saviour is just blowing in the wind," said Annie.

"Ain't that the truth?" I asked, sadly while readjusting my long black braid and recoiling it in a bun held firm with hair combs. My hair was so long that I could sit on it.

"Suse," said Annie. "If there was one person that I'd call a saint, it would have to be you. I think that you must have a special angel looking over your shoulder. I bet you'll be the best mother around. So don't worry about anything, cause you've got what it takes, in my book," said Annie.

I was pleased with my friend's kind words.

"You know Annie, I have always felt like I *do* have a guardian angel looking after me," I said.

"I always thank God for being there whenever I'm in need of a friendly ear." After a slight pause, I turned to Annie then continued with my voice lowered to a conspiratorial whisper.

"I wouldn't tell anyone else this but...seems as how you're my best friend and all... well Annie, sometimes when I dream, I see an angel and she talks to me," I revealed.

Annie was intrigued at my spiritual revelation and listened, patiently as I continued.

"It seems that whenever I am worried and don't have any answers from my family or friends, the 'Lady of the Light' -- that's what I call her, appears and she reassures me that everything is gonna be all right," I said.

Annie was filled with a rising admiration for Suse, and being so inspired that, for a moment, she was unable to express her feelings.

"Suse, that sure is a beautiful thing you just said. I wish I could meet someone like that in my dreams. I feel that God and his angels are present right here. You *are* a very special person, my dear, and I really feel honoured by being your best friend," said Annie.

"Don't you think that believing in God and his angels makes life a whole lot better for everyone?" I asked.

"You know, Suse, I feel the same way you do about God. But I experience Him, as only I can. Suse, you experience God's presence in a different way," said Annie.

I smiled and said, "I am glad that you believe in my revelation Annie, because it's all true. It really is! When God answers my prayers, according to His will, I feel so good that it encourages me to genuinely help others."

"It seems to me," concluded Annie, "that the virtue of love is only fulfilled when it is shared with others."

"Amen!" I added.

Just then, Demus strode down the hallway toward the kitchen. He walked up, greeted me with a kiss and wrapped his arms around me.

"Honey, I'm sure glad you are home, because I missed you. It gets lonely out there working, and lacking the comfort of my woman. Suse, to be honest, I started missing you as soon as I left the house this morning," said Demus.

I was overjoyed with his attention. I reached for Demus' hand and guided it to my swollen belly.

"You'll make a great father, Demus. I am so blessed. Can't you feel it move?" I asked.

"Put your hand over here," I directed. As I guided his hand to that area it seemed to 'pulsate' with life.

"Suse, I'm witnessing this miracle of life!" Exclaimed Demus, proudly.

"You know beautiful, if I can be half the person that you are, I'll consider myself truly blessed," said Demus, after he gave my tummy an affectionate squeeze.

"Mind your manners now Demus, and say 'hello' to our company," I said. Then I proceeded to pour him a cup of cocoa while he spoke to Annie.

"You are looking as pretty as ever Annie," he remarked. Annie smiled, shyly.

Demus stoked the fire of the pot-bellied stove, and sat in his favourite kitchen chair. I handed him his hot drink.

"Here you go dear, just the way you like it, with lot's of chocolate. It has a dab of whip cream on top, too," I added. At that moment, I leaned over and gave him a big kiss. How his face lit up!

"Why I do believe I've been kissed by an angel."

Annie smiled. "You know Demus, I believe that pretty wife of yours is an angel. She may deny it, but we know better, don't we?" Annie commented, with a delightful smile.

Demus laughed as he looked at me.

"Suse, don't look so modest. It's true."

Annie got up to prepare to leave. As dusk had fallen quickly, she had to return home to tend to her family. Demus offered her a ride home. He went outside to hitch the horse up to the buggy. Before Annie put on her hat on, she let down her long black hair to firmly reposition her hair bun. Thus, revealing her rich, Indian heritage. Annie and I said our goodbyes; and vowed to meet again... the Lord willing.

Upon his return from down the Johnson Road, Demus felt an urge to speak with me. Tonight, for some reason or another, he felt uncharacteristically unsure of himself. He moved his kitchen armchair beside me.

"Suse, tell me honestly, now. Do you really think that I would make a good father? I'd... I'd never done this before and..."

I gladly interjected.

"Demus, you're not the only one who's nervous here. It's my first time too, and I'll be the one suffering through the labour pains. But with the help of God and Cousin Sophie, we will have nothing to worry about. Along with Kitty Willis, Cousin Sophie is among the best of our midwives in New Road. Praise God! Why even, some of the white folk ask for their expertise!" I proudly exclaimed.

CHAPTER 6

DEMUS AND I, WERE soon blessed with our first child, name Noah. He turned out to be a sweet and healthy baby. Like any new parents, our life automatically revolved around him. Whenever his parents were busy working in the field or in the house, there were plenty of others around to keep an eye on him.

I was in the dinning room setting the table for dinner. A few minutes were left before the food was brought out. So, I sat down for a quick rest when Noah suddenly, let out a wail. I grinned. It was way of telling me that it was feeding time. I began to rise up from my chair when my mother, Mama Adeline had come in from the kitchen, and mentioned for me to remain seated.

"Just sit right there daughter and leave Noah to me. I'll feed him his Pabulum. You know how I just love feeding that little boy," said Mamma Adeline.

Demus listened to our discussion as to whose turn it was to feed Noah.

"Gee folks, when I was young, my mother was the only one around to take care of me. My boy is so lucky, he's got two mammas," said Demus. Mama Adeline chuckled as she picked up Noah and brought him to the dinner table. Now it was Demus' turn to jump up.

"Let me get the highchair, so my son can eat with the rest of the family," he said.

"All right Demus," said Mama Adeline, whose voice followed him into the kitchen.

"Just remember to bring Noah's hot Pabulum with you. I left it on the table to cool down a little." She turned her attention to the child squirming in her arms and laughed at his antics.

"Now we won't want you to burn your itsy bitsy mouth," she cooed in his ear.

All eyes were on Noah's cheerful, bubbling expression. He looked around the room and giggled. Everyone laughed in response.

As Noah was being fed, Demus and I were engrossed in an unusual topic of conversation.

"Suse, you know," said Demus. "This sounds strange but it sure is true."

"What's that dear?" I asked.

"Last week Dad heard tell, that an eight year old Chinese girl and her nine year-old boyfriend were the youngest and proudest parents ever," said Demus.

"At age what?" Mamma Adeline asked. She turned to look at Demus while trying hard to keep an eye on the impatient little Noah. He was kicking his chubby little feet in protest to the lack of attention. He didn't take too kindly to Mamma Adeline robbing him of his Pabulum.

"Believe it or not, Mama Adeline," replied Demus. "She was only eight and he was nine years old."

"Well, Bless my soul!" Mamma Adeline exclaimed.

"Now, see?" I remarked. "My best friend, Annie V. Johnson, and I were just talking about that. Children should be just that, 'children', and leave the baby making to us adults," I said, empathically.

"Oh, I'll drink to that Suse!" Demus exclaimed, with a big grin.

"Now, you just shush. And *you*... you don't even drink," I said, jokingly.

Many men grew dissatisfied with the monotony of family life, and pursued the excitement, or so they thought, of wine, women and song. But not Demus Smith. No siree! He contented himself with being one of the most spiritually rich men in the world. No amount of money, material goods or temptation could divert him from the love of his sweet Suse.

It is no wonder that the newspapers were advertising a 'cure' for hangovers. A weekly supply of tablets sold for 10¢ a box. The added use was a remedy for gastric complaints. The tablets reportedly stimulated bowel regulation.

As for a true cure for hangovers, oh well… that's another story. At the end of the 19th century, medical science was rudimentary, at best. The advertisement of natural medicine abounded. The nostrums or remedies were neither tried nor true, in most cases; but they had begun to invade the market. Consumers were left to fend for themselves.

As the years went by our family increased to five children: Noah, Helen, Adeline, Etta and Baby Joe. The family's size was surpassed only by our great joy and love for one another. After Demus was finished working in the field, I always looked forward to the family gathering. The evenings were my favourite time of day. Everyone retired to the parlour where we taught our children how to play the organ.

One morning in particular, as I cradled little Joe in my arms, I quietly sang to him the well-known lullaby, "Rock-a-bye baby on the tree top." I stopped singing as I watched the baby's eyes close. The soft sound of his little breath… I couldn't help but gaze sweetly on God's little miracle. Etta came up me, and threw her tiny arms around my neck. She kissed my cheek.

"Mama, you sing so beautiful. I love you," she said.

I looked at my daughter and reached out with my free hand to run my fingers down her long thick, curly braid. "I love you too, dear and don't you ever for get it!" I said.

"Mama," said Etta, as she contemplated posing a question.

"What, what kind of foods do baby birdies eat?"

"Well sweetie, let's see." I thought for a bit then continued, "they eat worms, ants, flies, caterpillars, grasshoppers, insect eggs and such."

Etta made a couple of ugly faces before exclaiming, "Phew! Ack! I'm sure glad that I'm a little girl, 'cause I get to eat people foods," she concluded, and ran off to play.

Demus had just finished hitching up the horse and buggy. He turned towards the window and waved goodbye. It was time for him to ride into town to buy hay and feed for the animals, as well as, run some errands for me.

Meanwhile, I allowed my mind to drift back to the time when I was a teenager, a little before the turn of the century. Since I was not permitted to sing in the white churches, I gladly sang in the many black churches that dotted the area.

On the other hand, the City of Halifax and Town of Dartmouth, still posted segregated signs that prohibited our people from walking on certain streets. And we were not to walk on Spring Garden Road or in the south end... period. Unless, of course for employment purposes.

As well, racial signs prohibiting us from entering parks such as: Halifax's Public Gardens, Point Pleasant Park or Citadel Hill Park, etc. Why... there were signs forbidding us from entering restaurants, hotels, barbershops and hair salons, etc. And don't make the mistake of asking to use *their* washrooms! May God have mercy on your soul!!!

In Halifax, one of our allotted washroom locations required a long, long walk or buggy ride straight uphill to the 'North Commons Public Washroom'. Often instead, we would pass by the homes of family and friends. We would be all *too* grateful for their charity.

In time, the park schedules allowed us entrance on weekends. I can remember singing in the Public Gardens, and other places simply for the pleasure of it. Folks would gather nearby to hear my voice. I often felt inspired as I looked around and saw the smiles on the listeners' faces. It was as if angels were hovering overhead, and enchanting the atmosphere with their love. This was at the time when George Dixon, the boxer from Africville had past away. The black communities throughout the province were still in mourning. Without realizing it, I began to sing one of my favourite Gospel hymns, 'The Old Rugged Cross'.

While in Dartmouth, Demus stopped in at the General Store. Gus, the proprietor, told the customers they had to use up their British currency. The Canadian Mint had recently turned out Canadian currency. As was the custom, folks milled about in discussion; before paying for purchases or having their items credited on tally sheets.

Vivian Willis

As Demus exited the store, he stopped to look around the property. "It's no wonder the grounds have to be kept so immaculate," he mumbled, while shaking his head in disgust. He could not imagine how a man could spend a whole 10¢ on a pack of cigarettes.

"What pleasure is there in all that puffing? And look at all these nasty butts thrown on the ground. Not to mention, that awful smell. Man, it's mighty, mighty funky! Um, Um, Ummm," said Demus, quietly.

He knew for certain, that his Suse would not tolerate any of that nonsense. "No siree!" Demus mumbled. "No siree!" Occasionally though, he did smoke a pipe in his parlour. But it didn't have the same funky odour as a cigarette.

As he loaded up the buggy, he had barely noticed a hair bun in the store window. Demus stepped closer to get a better look. He paused, to imagine it entwined in his wife's gorgeous hair.

"Excuse me, Gus? What's the price of the hair bun?" asked Demus.

"Ten cents, Demus. Do you want it wrapped?" Gus asked.

"Oh, yes, please and thank you," replied Demus.

"Is it Suse's birthday or a special occasion?" Gus quizzed, jokingly.

"No Gus, it's not her birthday or anything. It's just that my little Suse is always special to me," answered Demus, with the biggest smile.

"Wrap it up, please. It's a surprise… I hear that most women, love to be surprised," added Demus.

In the time before the World War I (1914-1918), women wore their hair long or braided and styled in a bun. It was held secure with hair combs or hair buns. As the war progressed, women were called to aid in the war efforts. For safety precautions, short hairstyles were created to avoid entanglement in the factory machinery.

The matter of dress, however, remained quite conservative or 'Victorian'. Long ankle-length skirts were worn with long sleeved blouses that covered the neck.

The undergarments consisted of thick-dark stockings worn with granny boots. They were ankle and calf length leather boots with front lacings. As well, gaiters or spats were worn for shoe protectors.

The gaiters were made of leather, felt or canvas. Oddly enough, gaiters were the colour of prunes. However, we called them 'prunella shoes'.

The main undergarments consisted of fancy corsets and petticoats. The laces of the corsets were often, pulled so tight, as to restrict proper lung functioning. The purpose of this practice was to affect an hourglass figure. Unfortunately, this custom, if worn continually, caused some women to suffer from fainting spells or much worse, from miscarriages.

Petticoats were a two-piece affair. The material was not at all constricting like that of the corset. The comfortable short top was sleeveless with an open neck.

Demus climbed into his buggy and headed home. Upon his return, he unloaded the buggy and stored the feed. He left the stable and headed for the barn. "One thing about animals," he mused, "they seemed to know when I'am coming to feed them." They'd nuzzled up to him and make soft, satisfied sounds.

After he finished the chores, he went into the house and was immediately greeted with the aroma of dinner. I was preparing the meal and singing softly when Demus entered the kitchen.

"What's for dinner honey?" Demus asked.

"Corned beef and cabbage," was my response. He rubbed his hands in anticipation then ran upstairs to change and wash up.

Before taking his seat, he greeted each of the children with a kiss and a hug. After supper, Demus joined me in front of the kitchen sink. Poor Demus was dog-tired from working from dawn to dusk. Yet, he still insisted on drying the dishes. I gave him an appreciative glance.

"Thanks for helping me with the dishes dear, with the children and all... some days I can hardly lift my feet... 'cause it seems like two days in one. I

don't know what I'd do without you. You really are my best friend," I commented.

Demus' response was, "You're mine too, Suse. No doubt about it, you are my best friend, and my lover." He leaned over and kissed me on the cheek.

"Suse, the other day at the Gus's store, he was telling everyone about the 'Titanic'. You know, you've heard of the unsinkable ship that... that sank," said Demus, eagerly.

"Any ship that is made by man is liable to sink, Demus. These people think that their inventions can... can never fail," I said, somewhat annoyed.

"Anyway," he continued, 'the Titanic' ran into an iceberg - right off the coast of Newfoundland. And get this; over 1500 people lost their lives. Only about 700 survivors! The rich were given the opportunity to live, and the poor – well... that's another story.

And get this; the ship wasn't even equipped with enough life jackets... or lifeboats. I guess 'cause it was supposed to be unsinkable!" he concluded. At this added piece in information, I sucked my teeth and rolled my pretty green eyes in dismay.

"Yeah Demus, just remember this, that only God respects everyone equally. Those rich folks," I mumbled, "always so big feeling. They think that their money is more powerful than... than the mighty Atlantic or, or God himself! Um, Um, Umm" I fumed.

"Suse, you know what else?" Demus asked, but not waiting for a response.

"Why, pretty near 150 bodies are buried here, right here!" he reported, rather proudly.

"Buried here, right here, I tell you," he repeated, enthusiastically.

"Here, here where?" I asked incredulously, obviously still upset over the unnecessary deaths.

"Demus, what in tarnation are you talking about? No white person is going to bury their dead in either of our New Road cemeteries," I said, emphatically.

"No Suse, you got it **all wrong**!" responded Demus, about to correct the huge misunderstanding.

"I mean, here in three Halifax cemeteries... here in Halifax!"

"Oh, oh well," I said, sounding a bit frustrated.

"Man, why can't you be more specific when you're sharing information?"

There we stood, looking at one another until we burst out laughing. Demus would always be Demus, and me? Well... I would be Suse.

The next day, Demus was toiling in the field, when he remembered the hair bun he bought yesterday. It was still in the pocket of his dungarees. He had been so tired the night before; it had completely slipped his mind.

This time, there was no way he'd forget. He trekked back to the house and slipped in the back door. I was in the kitchen, humming softly to myself. He snuck up behind me and wrapped his arms around my little waist. At first I was a little startled, but settled back against him. Demus pulled a package out of his pocket and placed it on the table in front of me.

"Yesterday, I brought you a present. Why don't you open it?" Demus said, proudly.

Well I couldn't wait. I anxiously ripped open the paper and held up the hair bun.

"Why Demus, it's lovely. How thoughtful of you. Why, it's not even my birthday or any thing!" I said, giggling like a schoolgirl.

"Because I love you," replied Demus. He watched me manoeuvre my hair around the hair bun.

"You look even more beautiful today than you did yesterday," Demus complimented.

"Oh Demus, that sounds so-o sweet. Now, to show my appreciation, I am going to make you a meal fit for a king!" I said, after I gave him a kiss.

"Every meal that you make is fit for royalty, dear. I really mean it," said Demus. He gave me another peck on the cheek before he headed out to his chores. I returned to the business of preparing 'my king' his meal.

The workday for Demus was always busy whether it was feeding the animals, ploughing the fields or harvesting the corps. A farmer's work is much like a woman's work – except that for her, it is *never* done!

No matter what type of task lay ahead, Demus always faced them in a chipper mood. Except for the time when the province legislated a change in driving policy. Drivers were to switch over, and drive on the right-hand side of the road within two months.

Vivian Willis

"Imagine!" Demus fumed, inwardly. "All those years of driving on the left-hand side of the road and now, in only two months – everybody has to go along with it... or be killed."

He walked in the farmhouse as the sun began its slow descent. He was anxious to smell the aroma of cooking. It thrilled Demus as the children ran into his arms and squealed with delight.

"What's for dinner dear?" Demus asked.

"Sure smells good, whatever it is. But that's not the current news. Actually," he added.

"Have you heard the current news? As we speak, a ship of about 500 Hindus are approaching the Halifax Harbour... refugees, I believe. The government calls it, 'The Asian Invasion'. The government is undertaking to return them back to India. Or at least, to keep them out of Canada."

Demus continued, "I say, that the Hindus should be allowed to stay. Seeings how we're bound to lose a whole lot more than 500 men, in the upcoming war that everyone's talking about. Frankly, I don't see the problem. If the truth be told, the government just doesn't want anymore Coloured folk here. Ya' see how they treat us... and the Indians, don't ya'?"

I gave him the 'all-knowing eye', and nodded in agreement.

"But baby, I'm hungry now and we'll continue this after supper," he concluded.

It was either myself or Demus who lit the kerosene lamps by pouring the paraffin oil into the reservoir. Often enough, I busied myself with darning, sewing or knitting items for family and friends. Then between the two of us, we would play the organ before reading the newspaper. Often when reading, he would drink a cup tea and smoke his pipe. I would allow positively no cigarette smoking in my home. No siree!

Demus' intuition was right. As of August 1914, Canada was, indeed, involved in the First World War. 'The No. 2 Construction Battalion', joined the Canadian forces as a segregated, black contingent unit. They didn't have much choice, because the government was giving them a hard time to enlist. Thankfully, Rev. William A. White (1874-1936), of the Second Baptist Church in New Glasgow served overseas with the battalion as the only back Chaplain in the

British Empire. The Mi'kmaq had also enlisted a total of 150 men in the Great War, as it was often called.

However, a horrific accident took place in Halifax Harbour a few years later. It was recorded as the first man-made explosion in history. On, December 6, 1917, at five minutes after 9:00 am, the French munitions ship, Mont Blanc was seriously overloaded with explosives when it collided with the Belgian Relief, the Imo. A horrific and angry fire erupted on the Mont Blanc. It was followed by gigantic explosion. This culminated with a massive tidal wave toward Dartmouth's Turtle's Cove Indian Settlement. In Halifax the death count was at 2000, the seriously wounded, 9000, and 200 were left without sight.

A day later, a sever blizzard battered Halifax, thereby hampering rescue efforts. Ironically, Cornwallis Baptist Church was the only area church left unharmed. It was utilized to shelter the injured homeless. The Town of Dartmouth lost about forty of its citizens. The resulting tidal wave practically levelled the Mi'kmaq school and its' settlement at Turtle's Cove. At least nine Native children and a number of adults lost their lives.

Hence, the survivors relocated to Shubenacadie. As they trekked mournfully along, their cries of lament lingered hauntingly in the air.

It seems that the black community of Africville, along the Bedford Basin was not spared, either. They arose to the challenge of rebuilding their damaged church and other property. Upon hearing of this current news, I had to view the devastation for myself. I remember being only able to nod my head and repeat, "My Lord... my Lord. What a morning!" In this instance, any information on blacks was not considered newsworthy.

As time went by, my family grew, but the enormity of the work took a strain on me physically and tragically. Almost yearly I found myself pregnant. However, this resulted in multiple miscarriages, stillbirths and enfant deaths. Believe it or not, I would have nineteen pregnancies. I lost nine babies, all within the space of about fourteen years. As well, in the 1930's, I would eventually, lose two grown daughters to consumption or tuberculosis.

The passage of time had caused me to comment that, "As God saw fit, He would truly bless my life with more children, in His divine wisdom. I really do believe that God must have a good reason for the loss of so many babies back up in Heaven with Him, because they were needed up there," I said, solemnly. In total, I had lost eleven children. My sad situation caused me to think on the words of an old poem.

> "Upon a Child
> Here a little pretty baby lies
> Sung asleep with lullabies
> Pray be silent, and not stir
>   Th' easy earth that covered her."[8]

As the years rolled on, God did bless me with three more children, who all survived: Pauline, Ruth and little Leota. During the last of these births, two older ladies, Kitty Willis and Lucy Beals, dear family friends, served as midwives.

As they monitored the latter stages of my last, successful pregnancy, we often sat in the parlour and reminisced about the early days in Nova Scotia.

"Thank goodness it's the mid 1920's and not the 1890's," Lucy remarked.

"Why is that Lucy, dear?" I asked.

"Back then Suse, when you were just a little girl, they **used** to sell slaves at the Market Square in Halifax. There was also a Public Slave Auction and a

Whipping Post. Hm, this slave-dirt all began when these cities were built. You know something else? Those slaves ought to be respected. Um hmm, 'cause they made a clearer path for **us**," reported Lucy, proudly.

"They sho' did," I said, in agreement.

"Lucy and Kitty, you know something else? I **do** remember seeing that slave-dirt. Oh yes, I was small, but I saw things. I felt scared at hearing those hellish sounds... auction sounds. **All** that hollering and screaming. It chilled the bones. The smell of... of" I hesitated. Of fresh blood... just sickening, just sickening. Oh, I was **so-o terrified.**

Mom Suse: Matriarch of the Preston area Black Communities

I thought they were gonna *whup* me and Mama, too… and, and take *us* away." I admitted, almost in tears.

"You fellas, I sure was a witness 'cause I'm a lot older than the two to you," said Kitty, pausing to catch her breath. She lowered her voice and spoke real soft.

"Oh, I have *seen* some things, um hmmm, I have *seen* some nasty… cruel, things," repeated Kitty.

"You know something else?" Kitty whispered.

"They whupped their *own kind*, too, 'cause *he* spoke out. Um hmm, told them that it wasn't right," added Kitty, with a pained, faraway expression.

"They did him *some* bad! Oh, like the words the Negro Spiritual says, 'Nobody Knows the Trouble I've seen!" Kitty concluded.

"I think, I think… its time for some pleasant talk," said Lucy, quietly.

After a moment, I rose to the challenge and I spoke.

"They built the 'Home for Coloured Children', a few years ago, in 1921. It was a positive thing. You know that our girls are schooled in domestic trades. I mean they can't become nurses or anything. It seems like society is afraid that we might succeed. Hm well, the Home was founded by, Mr. J.A.R. Kinney. In fact, my grandparents, Annie and Daniel Cain, worked on the Orphanage farm in the 1840's. That's where they met." I reported, proudly.

"In the area of Domestic Science, they teach nutrition, canning, cooking, home economics, and hygiene," said Kitty, just beaming.

"Did you fellas hear that a law was finally passed forbiddin' the use of alcohol?" Lucy asked.

"I do believe," she added, "that it's about time somebody got it right."

"You know… life is a bit easier for women now. I think that we can vote at age twenty-one." I paused to release a heavy sigh. Then with the shake of my head, I quickly added.

"Oh, I don't think that means our folk, no siree," I said, rather sarcastically. I pondered the thought, for a moment. Then, with a sudden grab of my swollen belly, I let out a moan.

"Oh, I think," I said, through clenched teeth, "my water has broken."

"Hold on Suse, we'll get you upstairs, fast," said Kitty.

She was all business.

"Lucy, please get some hot water, some cord, and bring it upstairs," directed Kitty.

A short while later, the labour pains intensified.

"I can see the baby's head Suse, I can see the baby's head," Kitty repeated. "Push harder," she instructed.

I took deep breaths. The baby started to emerge from the womb.

Then I began to sweat, profusely. No matter how many babies I had, it ***never*** got easier. Gripping the bed sheets, I screamed out, "God help me! God help me!"

At this point, I saw a Heavenly Light in the form of a beautiful Lady hovering over the bed. The Lady looked down and smiled at me.

Her reassuring gesture helped me to manage the pain. As Kitty gently smacked the newborn's derriere, I whispered, Thank you, Lady."

Kitty thought that I was thanking her and replied, "No need to thank anyone dear, you're doing fine and you have a healthy baby girl."

I smiled at the beautiful baby then drifted into a deep and pleasant sleep. While I was dreaming, the 'Lady of the Light', reappeared in my midst as a shimmering light.

"How is my baby girl? Is there something wrong?" I asked.

"She's fine and healthy," the Lady spoke in a harmonious tone.

"You are one great woman to have such a blest family," said the Lady. Her voice caused me to again, fall into a dreamless sleep.

When I awoke, Demus was at my bedside, holding my hand.

"We have a cute baby-girl Suse," he said excitedly.

"All the children are downstairs waiting to see their new sister."

"Can we call her Leota?" I asked, weakly.

"Sure, I imagine so," Demus replied. "It's a marvellous name."

"That's what the Lady said. The beautiful Lady told me to call our new daughter, Leota," I concluded.

Chapter 7

It was the late 1920's; Mom Suse was traveling to Cherry Brook to see her dear old dad, John Bundy. She and her siblings would take turns tending to him, as his wife had past a few years ago. Mr. Bundy still looked at Suse as his 'little girl'.

"Suse," asked Dad. "Don't you think you're doing too much work? A woman's got to slow down sometime."

"Dad, I know how much you love me and with Mama gone and all, but... I'm, I'm just fine. And, I don't think that I'll be having any more babies. So, that's one less thing to worry about. And I've always found that my body rewards me with good health when I treat it sensibly," I replied.

I helped to cook his meals, wash the clothes and clean the house. Dad spent most of the day sitting in the parlour listening to his 'new' radio. He bought it some years ago, but to him, it was always 'new'. In fact, Dad was overjoyed to hear the first hockey game in the early '20's, via radio broadcast.

While I worked around the house, he filled me in on current and past events. It was a special time for both of us. Dad mentioned that a few years back in 1927, he heard that Babe Ruth was paid a yearly salary of $70,000... the highest paid baseball player ever. There arose a pride in his voice when he mentioned that the Bluenose Schooner was ingrained on the Canadian dime around 1921.

But he wasn't too sure, because his memory sometimes failed him, so he said. But to me, Dad's memory seemed just fine.

"Suse, Did you know that our domestic workers were often paid only $1.00 per day, and most of them were actually, no more than indentured servants? Nobody in Canada wants to admit that there was slavery here so they smoothed it over with the term, 'indentured servants'. Well, for those wages, they might as well have called it 'slavery', for slave labour," remarked Dad.

I just sat back and nodded. My father was blest with a great memory. It was time for me to listen, and learn a thing or two.

"Little Suse, I recall hearing that back in 1887, the new Los Angeles subdivision of Hollywood, sold the land for $150.00 per acre. Just imagine how much profit that land would be worth now!" He exclaimed.

My older children were grown and had started their own families. Noah, the eldest son married his childhood sweetheart, Rebecca. Our eldest daughter, Helen was soon to be married. Hence, in terms of responsibility, the younger ones, still at home, took their rightful places.

One morning, when I scooped the cream out of the milk can, Joe and Pauline walked into the kitchen, still rubbing the sleep out of their eyes.

"Good morning, Mama," Pauline spoke softly in her sweet, 'little girl's voice'.

Then little Joe hugged, yawned and wished me a good morning.

"Good morning to you too, my little angels," I replied.

I turned and added, "Perhaps, you're awake enough to go out and collect some eggs from the chickens, my darlings. Don't forget to wash up first, though."

"Yes Mama, you know that I don't mind helping you out," said Pauline. She washed up, changed her clothes, reached for the basket and headed out the rear door.

"Now for you young man, I think your father needs help with the livestock this morning," I commented.

"All right Mama," said the little child, dutifully. Little Joe washed up, changed and headed out towards the barn.

"Morning Papa, I've come to help you clean up and milk the cows," said little Joe.

"That's just fine son." Demus said with a smile. "I was wondering when you were getting out here. I was afraid you'd sleep the whole day through." Demus stepped aside and led his son's hands to the cow's udder. Little Joe sat on the milking stool and tried to emulate the same rhythmic motion he saw his father use.

Demus stood over him and smiled at his son's valiant efforts in milking 'ole Bessie.

The scene took him back to when he was a child, learning the same techniques from his dad. Once he realized that little Joe was milking properly, he left him alone and herded the other cows out to pasture.

When he returned, his son stood proudly beside a pail full of milk. Demus grinned and patted little Joe lightly on the shoulder.

"Okay son, it looks like you've done a mighty fine job of milking 'ole Bessie. I'll finish here, if you go out and collect some of that freshly chopped wood," concluded Demus.

He picked up the pail and poured it into the sterilizer while little Joe ran out to complete his chores.

Chapter 8

It seemed that an unseen hand had pulled the plug on the financial pulse of New York's Stock Exchange. This 'unforeseen' event occurred on September 3, 1929. Perhaps, a phantom plummeted the economy down an invisible well. Things were so bad, that it was questionable whether stocks could be revived.

In North America the banks had to close down. Thereby, forcing its citizens to accept, the fact, that their money wasn't worth a 'red cent'! Unfortunately, several 'previously rich men' snuffed out their own lives.

Here in Canada, the government made provisions to employ single men. But this was merely subsistent living. During the dark days of the Great Depression, a total of one million Canadians, found themselves, chronically unemployed. In fact, the Maritimes recorded the highest unemployment rate in the country.

In Halifax, a camp was stationed at the fortress of Halifax Citadel. It housed 300 men who worked for a dastardly 20¢ per day. This was, of course, quite outrageous! In addition, they received military rations and shared accommodations.

Starving Haligonians could be found standing in the bread lines, literally begging for food while most living in farming communities were a little better off.

It was also more feasible for country and city folk with wood stoves and oil lamps. The oil lamps gave off excellent light and warmth, but, at times, the fumes were notorious.

Back in New Road, Mom Suse's young daughter Pauline was preparing to accompany her mother to town. Mom Suse's customers often gave her clothing and other items to help support her family.

These gifts were always accepted, graciously. Whatever did not fit her family was sent to others. This generosity was one of the reasons why Mom Suse was so blest, despite all of the families' tribulations. The old adage remains, 'What goes around, comes around'.

Pauline and I approached our first customer of the day but our anticipation of a quick sell evaporated when we heard the voice on the other side of the door.

"We don't want none. My man's gone, so I ain't buying nothing!" she said, in an irritated tone.

The door opened a crack. The young woman shook her head vigorously to reinforce her statement. Without acknowledging this woman, we left the porch in the hopes of greener pastures and headed back to the buggy.

"Don't let that woman get you down Pauline," I said, compassionately. "She probably has had a real hard time of it --- all by herself."

We climbed into the buggy. Just then, I hesitated and looked back at the house.

I exclaimed, "I can't leave that poor girl like that." I reached into the back of the buggy to pull out a jar of blueberry jam.

"Here Pauline," I said. while handing her the jar.

"Give this to the lady, *free of charge*, and tell her that our prayers are with her. We hope that her man comes back soon."

"I will Mama," responded Pauline. "I think this is what she needs right now, some kindness."

Pauline took the jam up to the house and rang the doorbell. The face re-appeared in the window.

"I said, I don't want none; now get going or else!" Pauline took one step forward and spoke in a loud, gentle voice to the troubled woman.

"Ma'am, I want to *give* you this jar of blueberry jam... to sort of help make you feel better."

"You want to *give* it to me, *free of charge*?" The woman asked, in surprise.

"That's right ma'am. My mom said it might cheer you up a little. It may be none of our business, but you seem a little down today."

Pauline waited… the door opened and a small, emaciated woman stepped outside. Her face formed a smile, as Pauline handed her the jar.

"My name is Sarah Pringle. What's yours?" Unconsciously, she held the jar to her bosom.

Pauline introduced herself, and was obviously overjoyed in the change of the woman's attitude.

"Would you like to meet my mother?" Pauline asked.

"Anyone who is as nice as you and your mother are welcome here," said Sarah, unable to hide the excitement in her voice.

Pauline and Sarah went out to where Mom Suse was patiently waiting, with that 'all-knowing' smile.

"Mama, I'd like to introduce you to my new friend, Sarah Pringle. Sara, this is my mother." Pauline said, proudly.

I extended my hand to the woman.

"Hello Mrs. Pringle, my name is Mrs. Smith. How are you doing?" I asked.

"I'm doing all right now that I've met such nice, generous folks as you two. I now regard you as friends," replied Sarah.

"I'm glad you feel that way," I said. "You can never have too many friends, in these lean times."

"I don't have many friends at all. It seems that I just don't get out and meet people anymore. I don't have much to offer, but you're welcome to come in for a cup of tea before you continue on your journey," said Sarah, graciously.

"Thanks very much," I replied smiling. "I think a cup of tea would be perfect, especially with the nip in the air today."

The three women walked towards the kitchen. As they walked in, both mother and daughter noticed that the house was in disarray. Sarah picked up on it immediately and tried to explain.

"I'm sorry about the mess, but I've been feeling very lonely since my husband left to look for work, and I don't have the energy or the desire to care, anymore," explained Sarah.

"Don't you worry about it none, I said softly and put my arm around the distraught woman's shoulder. I'm just glad you feel better with us here," I added.

"Loneliness can be an awful thing," commented Sarah. Her voice was filled with remorse.

"When there is no work and little to eat, you seem to lose your love of living," said a disconsolate Sarah.

Sarah stopped short and put her hand to her lips, but it was too late. Her body was racked with grief. She tried to cover her face from the visitors, but the tears could not wait. I attempted to comfort the distraught woman.

"Now don't cry child! I know things are tough now, but they are bound to get better," I said, with compassion.

As the tears ceased, Sarah sniffed and looked around, apologetically.

"I'm sure glad I met you fellas. I've been so depressed lately, I just don't want to live anymore." The tears made another unwanted appearance.

"How long has your husband been out of work?" I asked, sympathetically.

"It's been almost a year now," said Sarah, between the sobs.

"Please, don't cry Sarah. I have a feeling that everything is going to be all right and I bet your husband will be back soon with some good news," I encouraged.

"Do you really think so?" Sarah asked as she rubbed her eyes and regained her composure. She tried to smile, "I think I'll get up now and brew some tea, like I promised."

"Sarah, you are still blest, you know. Why, I just heard a real sad story about several women who were living in abject poverty. Their husbands had gone to look for work, too. The women and their children were literally... starving. Not knowing what else to do, the mother's took the leaves of the rhubarb and boiled them for food. Unbeknownst to them, the leaves were poisonous. Needless to say... **they all died**. So, so you just sit there, and remember to thank God for your **very life**, and take it easy," I said.

I helped the woman back to her chair.

"Pauline and I will make the tea, honey. Don't you worry about a thing, it will work out fine, just you wait and see," I remarked.

"The tea's in the cupboard over the sink," said Sarah, as she pointed to the sink half filled with dishes.

Without a word, Mom Suse walked to the area indicated and opened the cupboard. A tea tin sat on an, otherwise, empty shelf. The desolate look of the cupboard reflected the owner's life, all too well. When Mom Suse saw the empty shelf with the lonely tin, her eyes welled up with tears.

She stood there for a moment desperately trying to compose herself, before proceeding to boil the water.

"I'm sorry, I don't have much to offer beside the tea," said Sarah, regretfully.

"Since my husband's been out of town, the money has been scarce. I have a little garden outside that keeps me fed, but not much else," added Sarah.

"That's all right, dearie," I said cheerfully.

"Pauline, go and see if we have any cookies in the buggy, please and thank you."

I gave her a wink. Pauline understood. She waited until Sarah's head was turned and winked back.

Pauline returned just as Mom Suse was pouring the tea into the three cups that she had surreptitiously washed.

"We have plenty Mama. You always pack too big a lunch," commented Pauline. She then, pulled out enough sandwiches and cookies to satisfy the three of us.

"This is just like Christmas," cried Sarah, joyfully.

"I don't know how to thank you," she added.

I'm glad you're feeling better Sarah, anything we can do to help you – just let us know," I said.

The once dismal atmosphere dissipated. The three women chatted as though there was 'nothing wrong with the world'. Time passed by, way too quickly. 'Tea time' was over.

"I'm sorry, I clean forgot about the time. You folks, probably have to get back to business," noted Sarah.

"My dear, it's been a great pleasure to spend some time with you. You're a very nice lady and I'm glad we met you," I replied.

"That's right," agreed Pauline. "You're a real sweet lady and I'm equally glad to meet your acquaintance."

"It was so nice of you both to come to my side, just when I needed a shoulder to cry on," said Sarah, as she showed Pauline and I to the door.

"In these tough times nice people like you two are hard to find. You're welcome back, anytime," encouraged Sarah.

We'd be delighted to come back and visit again," I said. I leaned over and kissed Sarah's cheek. Pauline gave her little hug.

We waved one last time, and took off down the road.

"Pauline, since we were guests in her home I didn't want to embarrass her. But when I was in the kitchen, I noticed that the poor woman had nothing to eat. Absolutely, nothing! I'm glad we packed enough lunch this morning that we could share with someone. It just breaks my heart to see anyone in that awful position," I remarked.

"Mama, we may not have much ourselves, but when you see someone living in dire straights, well… it just breaks my heart, too. That's why it's important to share what little we have with those less fortunate than ourselves," said Pauline.

"Spoken like a true Christian," I exclaimed. I turned to Pauline and found myself fighting back the impulse to hug her.

"You make me really proud of you," I commented.

"Mama, I learned *everything* from you and Papa," said Pauline.

"I have watched the both of you treat total strangers with respect. I feel truly blest to have great parents."

"Pauline, we've had such a good start to the day," I said.

"I thought it might be a good idea to see Mrs. Wheeler. She has always been a good customer and I would like to tell her about poor Sarah. Maybe she can do something for her," I stated.

"What a great idea Mama. Maybe Mrs. Wheeler will be able to hire Sarah to clean her house or something," added Pauline.

"Great minds think alike," I laughed as I spoke.

"Pauline, I was thinking of exactly the same thing."

We stopped our horse and buggy outside an immaculate looking farmhouse. It was a little ways off from Sarah's home.

"Well, here we are," I said. "I hope that she's home," I added, as we approached Mrs. Wheeler's residence.

"I can see her from the curtains Mama," said Pauline, excitedly.

"She must be expecting us. This probably means our first sale of the day."

As we reached the driveway, Mrs. Wheeler came out of the house to greet us. She was a thin, frail lady with a cane, a pleasant disposition and a disarming smile. And most importantly, Mrs. Wheeler was not only Mom Suse's favourite customer, but in times of need, a dedicated friend.

"Hi folks!" Mrs. Wheeler greeted us halfway up the driveway.

"I was wondering when you were going to be dropping by. I'll need some extra blueberries today because I want to make some pies. I hope you've got them."

"Oh, we have them. In fact, the buggy is loaded with them. We're ready for you," I answered.

"Well, come inside," said Mrs. Wheeler. "And bring the blueberries with you. I have some sandwiches ready and there is tea brewing on the wood stove. I think I'll take three big baskets."

Pauline and I carried the baskets of blueberries into the house behind Mrs. Wheeler.

"I'm glad you two were finally able to get here." Mrs. Wheeler continued talking as she led us into the kitchen.

"I 'am looking forward to doing some baking this evening."

"I wish all our customers felt that way. Most of them are downright mean the way they treat us. You'd think we were selling them mud pies instead of berries. Some of them call us 'dusky' and 'swarthy', **everyday, everyday**. Really now... there is no need," I said, feeling frustrated.

"There's no accounting for people's tastes here," said Mrs. Wheeler. I told her that we just finished 'tea time' with Sarah Pringle. I explained the lady's plight to her.

Mrs. Wheeler shook her head, then exclaimed.

"The poor dear. I have a little extra food in here. Why don't you take it to her on your way back home?" Mrs. Wheeler suggested.

"That's really nice of you. She does need some food. There are too many in her situation," I remarked.

Mrs. Wheeler nodded in sympathy and recalled, "I can remember when I was young. It wasn't easy for my husband and I either."

I had to agree. "We had it tough too, when Demus and I started out. That's why I try to help out others whenever I can. Uh hm, we all know that Canadian Geese fly south for the winter and, that they fly in the form of a 'V'. Why is that? Because when each bird flaps its wings, there is an updraft to support the bird behind. When they honk and fly, it serves to encourage the front flyers to stay on course and maintain speed. During these Depression years, it's the geese that show us that together we must fly higher and further, rather than to go it alone," I concluded.

After more cordial conversation, Pauline and I said our farewells and mounted the buggy.

As we drove away Pauline said, "That was nice of Mrs. Wheeler, she doesn't even know the poor woman, and she is offering up all this food."

"That's why the lady is one of my best customers and friends,'" I commented.

The Smith team promptly drove the provisions to Mrs. Pringle, who stood at her doorway, and cried with joy. Sarah gratefully accepted the job as a domestic for Mrs. Wheeler.

"Thank God for good friends... old and new," said Sarah, happily.

While approaching the next house, Pauline and I heard a dog barking in the front yard.

"Now what do *you* people want around here?" A lady appeared from nowhere and looked on them with murderous eyes. "If you don't leave here right away, I'll sic my dog on ya'. I mean it, now – clear off!"

The woman's mean disposition threatened to destroy our good mood. Problem solved! We moved on to the next house. As the Depression stretched on, money became harder to obtain. Nice people became vindictive, and often laced their comments with cruel sarcasm.

At the next house, a little boy playing on a swing greeted us.

"Well, little boy, how are you?" I asked. "Is your mommy home?"

"My mommy's at work lady, but granny's here. Want me to get her?" The little boy asked.

"That would be mighty nice of you, young man," I replied.

The little blonde boy in his blue overalls and checkered shirt ran into the house to fetch her. Minutes later, a kind-looking elderly woman emerged from the house wearing a full-length paisley apron.

"What can I do for you folks?" she asked

"Were wondering, if you'd like to buy some fresh blueberries?" I asked, kindly.

"How much are they?" The lady inquired as she corralled her grandson.

"Fifty cents a quart. The larger quarts sell for sixty cents. How many would you like?" I asked, in a most professional tone.

"Oh, I'll take two regular quarts. Be right back with the money, though," she replied.

The grandmother went into the house and re-appeared with a dollar bill firmly clenched in her hand.

"Here Alfie, take this dollar bill to the nice people and bring me back the blueberries. We're, gonna have fresh blueberry pie for supper tonight!" Exclaimed the grandmother.

Alfie took the dollar bill from his grandmother and walked happily with it to the buggy. I promptly exchanged the dollar with two regular baskets. Pauline stepped down and helped him into the front yard where the grandmother collected the baskets.

"Now thank the nice ladies for the blueberries, Alfie," said the grandmother. The young lad suddenly turned shy and hid behind his granny's skirt. The old lady chuckled.

"Come again ladies, there is always a shortage of fruit in this house; blueberries are our favourite," she informed.

As they approached the following house, Mom Suse and daughter Pauline heard sounds of hammering. Mom Suse raised her voice in a greeting. A woman raised her head from the veranda and returned the greeting.

"What can I do for you, friend?" The lady asked.

"We are selling fresh wild blueberries," I said, in response.

"We can't buy any today," was the reply.

"My husband is off doing odd jobs until he finds something permanent. So we're only scraping by from one day to the next. I try to keep busy 'round here by keeping the place fixed up and tidy; but it is tough and I don't know where the next meal is coming from," she reported.

"Cheer up, dear. Things are bound to get better. I heard the government has some work programs going on that's bound to have some jobs down here sooner or later," I said, thoughtfully.

"I'll believe it when I see it lady, for now we're just hoping to make ends meet," replied the woman.

"We know how it is ma'am, were in the same boat." I responded, assuredly

"See you!" The woman said, before she resumed her hammering.

"Pauline, It's all in a day's work. We'll just have to take it in stride and hope that tomorrow will be better. We have get on to our next customer," I concluded.

Mom Suse was busy cleaning up her dad's place in Cherry Brook. As usual, he was anxious to share the latest news flash with her.

"Suse, I wonder where on earth did the City of Toronto find the money to build. I speaking about a huge hockey complex like Maple Leaf Gardens. And all this, happened in the middle of the Depression?" Dad inquired. People are starving, out of work, and they are building? Hm, now granted, construction *is* good for jobs," added Dad.

"Suse, I'll bet you'll be glad to hear this one, the government has taken control of the sale of liquor. Ya' know the purpose? It's a money racket thing," he remarked.

"I believe, but don't quote me now, that the beginning of income taxes, was the same year as 'The Halifax Explosion' – that it, it was going to be the ruin of us all!" Dad exclaimed.

"Oh, Dad, you are so dramatic, that's why I love you so," I said, sweetly.

Dad smiled but kept on talking. He was glad to have someone with whom he could make conversation. Even if, most of the time, she was busy. At his age, company was the key factor.

"Suse, you know when folks say, 'that was the Real McCoy'?" Dad asked.

"Yes, Dad," I answered, curiously.

Vivian Willis

"McCoy was a real person, a Coloured man. Yes siree! Elijah McCoy was born in 1871, in Colchester, Ontario. He was the inventor of things like the apparatus for oil engines to be used on trains and in factories. People make imitations – people will always make imitations, but there will never be anything like...." Dad commented.

"The Real McCoy," I playfully finished his sentence.

"Dad, you're something else. You're *my* Real McCoy", I added.

As the Great Depression came to a close, more grief was about to plague the Smith household. In the 1800's, the disease of Tuberculosis or commonly called (consumption) was the primary cause of death, worldwide. It was a highly contagious bacterial lung infection causing the lungs to abscess and scar.

These lean years introduced folks to a whole new way of life. Many had their first experience with poverty – abject poverty for some. Folks contended with crowded living conditions, inadequate diet and poor personal hygiene. The malady of consumption could be contracted through sneezing, coughing and the spitting of chewed tobacco (a very common practice).

In the mid 1930s Papa Demus and Mom Suse lost two of their eldest daughters to this wretched disease. It was Adeline, who first succumbed... followed by dear Etta. Consumption ravaged the body slowly and painfully. One would ask, "How much more could Mom Suse have taken?" But she continued to ask God for strength. When received, she held it in the palm of her hands. Mom Suse *never* cursed God for her losses.

She understood that everyone has their own 'cross' to bear, and she bore hers the only way she knew; like a good soldier in Christ. Who can know the will of God?

She never questioned His leading in her life; Mom Suse simply followed. It is in times like this, that the soul is embraced with the tranquility of God.

During the Depression years, she was, undoubtedly, a beacon of light in her community. When some folks were full of doom and gloom, Mom Suse was the voice of inspiration, no matter how difficult things became.

Mom Suse: Matriarch of the Preston area Black Communities

As the years came to a close, World War II became the dominant concern. The demand for food and business began picking up on their farm. The economy was finally on an upsurge. Again, Canada went off to war. Once again, the authorities attempted of keep blacks out of the forces, but not for long. None can stop the will of God! Blacks joined all services in the war. Our men were accompanied by, Chaplain, Dr. William P. Oliver (1912-1989).

Dr. Oliver ministered at three area churches, Cornwallis Baptist Church, Beechville Baptist Church, and Lucasville Baptist Church. As well, there were over 250 Mi'kmaq who also enlisted in WWII.

Mr. Bundy continued looked forward to Suse's visits. He longed for her sweet company and sweet presence. It was as if, she understood the trials he faced in old age. His radio became a constant companion, but no matter how effective the technology, nothing could replace the personal bond.

"Suse, there is one thing that the federal government got right," said Dad, with gratitude.

"What's that?" I asked.

"It was the mid-1920's, when they instituted Old Age Pension. Without that, I don't know how I'd manage.

There truly is a God!" he stated.

"Suse, remember the Dionne quintuplets, born in '34?" Dad questioned. "It's a shame that the Ontario government took those babies from their parents with the excuse that they didn't understand English. That doesn't make a lick of sense. I reckon, that the officials didn't have a clue about French, either. You know, It's a crying shame how they put those babies on display... just like a sideshow. Took all control away from the parents," said Dad, mournfully.

"Took their money, too," he added.

"Dad, do you know another word for capitalism?" I quizzed. Not waiting for his response, I quickly answered.

"It's called greed. Plain, and simple," I replied.

"Um hm, honey," said Dad.

"And guess what? They say that in '35, the last Haligonian legally executed was a thirty-nine year old Coloured man named Daniel P. Sampson. um the thing is... he was retarded," noted Dad.

"Well, what was his crime, did you hear that?" I quizzed.

"I believe that he was charged with the murder of two children... in a blueberry patch. Imagine that!" he added.

"In a blueberry patch?" I repeated.

"Sure they got the right man?"

"That's not all," Dad noted. "They say that the last Nova Scotian to be executed was an Indian from Shelburne County. An Everett Farmer, they say he died in '32, for the murder of... I don't think they mentioned that part. No, I don't remember hearing or reading that," said Dad.

"What else is new in Nova Scotia? The black man and the Indians always used as scapegoats. Well, I guess... somebody takes the fall," I said, in disgust.

No sooner had things picked up for the Smith family, then tragedy reared its ugly head. Papa Demus was diagnosed with full-blown Diabetes. And in time, this disease would claim his eyesight.

Although the family was devastated by the sudden turn of events, a positive spirit came to the forefront. Family members chipped in and continued to make the farm a viable operation.

Papa Demus was so-o depressed at losing a good portion of his independence. He needed constant comforting from his wife.

Being a proud man, and the principal breadwinner of the family... this news had 'cut him', so to speak, right through his heart. It was a wound that only time, and the Good Lord could heal.

When Mom Suse visited her dear old dad, it wasn't all work and no play. Since her siblings were so competent, many times his meals were cooked and portions kept in the icebox. As well, the housework was already done. It was on these occasions that she joined her dad in the parlour. They simply enjoyed one another's company.

"Sweetie, I'm sure Demus told you about the mob incident of '37. It took place in Trenton," said Dad, rather seriously.

"Dad, I can't say that I remember. Sounds rough though," I commented.

"Yeah, well you know... some prejudice thing... ah discrimination. That's what the young folks call it now – discrimination. Things took a vicious turn when a white mob practically destroyed the home of a black man," recalled Dad.

Mom Suse: Matriarch of the Preston area Black Communities

"Why? Just because... because they could?" I asked, rather perturbed.

"Dad, your memory is incredible. You remember everything that you hear and read. I wish mine was so sharp," I added.

"Suse, your memory is more incredible than mine, you silly girl." Dad said, jokingly.

"Whoa, wait a minute - we're going off topic," said Dad. "Now, back to Trenton and my story. The reason behind the angry mob is that the black man's home was in a white neighbourhood. And Suse, to top it off, apparently, the homeowner was arrested for assaulting a white woman. And guess what? All this while defending his own property," commented Dad, in anger.

"But, I believe that accusation was trumped up," he added.

"Dad, and they say that racism is mainly in the states. Then they should come on up here, to Nova Scotia!" I exclaimed.

"Umm, too many white folk in Canada are wading knee-deep in denial. It's high time for them to "get their minds right!" said Dad, with great conviction.

"Just accept the past to clear the wrongs," added Dad. "... And it's their painful past, too."

"Let's change the subject, Dad. It's no use getting all riled up," I suggested.

"Alright. Um, now, would you agree that the invention of the nylon stockings is a good thing?" asked Dad. He didn't wait for my response.

"It seems that male bank robbers took a shine to them too."

"What? How's that?" What on earth would they be using nylons for?" I asked, rather puzzled.

"Well, ha, ha, ha, the robbers put a stocking on their heads as a disguise," answered Dad, almost ready to bust open with laughter.

"Wait a minute, Dad," I said.

"Let me understand this, you mean... like a sleeping cap with the leg to mid-thigh knotted on the top? Like what we black folks wear to bed?" I questioned, with a big grin.

"Honey, those men are some simple... they're comical, that's all I've got to say," remarked Dad.

"Say, Suse, have you ever heard of the word, 'ghetto'?" Dad inquired.

"No, I can't say I have. How is it spelt? G-E-T-O-E?" I asked.

"Actually, I believe the right spelling is, G-H-E-T-T-O," corrected Dad.

"Oh… well, what is it and where is it?" I asked.

"Suse, it isn't a thing, it's an area in Warsaw Poland that Nazi Germany build. It's supposed to hold about 500,000 Polish Jews. They were relocated into this walled community," replied Dad.

"Dad, I would call that a 'prison' not a community. Imagine, looking at the four walls and then walking outside to another set of four walls. Oh no, no you don't," I added … that would just make me c-r-a-z-y! I remarked.

"Honey, maybe that was the whole idea of the plan. Mind control!" Added a wise old Dad.

"Maybe the Nazi's felt guilty and didn't want to look at the folks they had sorely persecuted," I stated.

"Suse, you know, 'that the human heart can't be trusted', he paraphrased. Just like the Good Book says in *Jeremiah 17:9."

"Amen," I concluded. "Amen!

*Taken from the King James Version of The Holy Bible

Chapter 9

It was a kerosene-fed fire! Although, not intentionally. It didn't take long for the first part of the house to go up in flames. They leaped real high, as if for joy, and danced in living colour! This fire wasn't quite satisfied. Oh no… not just yet. It had hoped to devour everything in sight. By the time the Volunteer Fire Department had arrived, the flames were already quenched. Her gluttonous appetite had been satisfied. OH, you could hear the crackling noises of the fire as she 'smacked her chops' – leaving only the smoldering ashes for her burial ground.

Thank God that there were no fatalities. The simmering ashes became a cemetery for the Smith families' treasured memories and prized possessions. That was the fire of the early 1940's. Despite years of accumulated tragedies, Mom Suse and her family never gave up. They built another house with the help of family and friends.

After settling in on evening, Demus and I were taking a stroll down memory lane to reminisce about the 'good old days'.

"Ya' know Suse," said Demus, "I remember the times when you and I paid a visit to Cousin Sophie's house. We used to listen to the boxing matches on her battery-operated radio."

Cousin Sophie was the midwife to all of Mom Suse's children, except the last three. Before Cousin Sophie's time, Kitty Willis was one of the first true midwives in New Road. She was a grandmother to Mr. James Willis, Pauline's husband.

Mom Suse was glad to hear Papa Demus mention Cousin Sophie because the memories warmed her heart.

"Yes, Demus, Cousin Sophie was one the best midwives around. There was hardly any baby that she didn't deliver – sho' was a busy woman, my, my, my," I said, with pride.

"Suse, some of our greatest times with Cousin Sophie were when we heard the matches of the great boxer, Joe Louis. You remember his nickname? 'The Brown Bomber'. Do you remember his first fight with that German fella, Max Schmeling? That was back in '32, in Norfolk, Virginia. That was, I think -- a year after the Lindbergh kidnapping. Louis lost the fight in the 12th round," Demus commented, sadly.

"Demus, you know, if I remember correctly, Nazi Germany was using that young boxer to promote their hated ideas. Even in America, the radio announcers, and newspapers had Schmeling listed as a Nazi.

That young fella probably didn't have Hitler and his henchmen to think about. I'll bet he just wanted to be a boxer," I remarked.

"Nothin' but good old propaganda – they'd propagate anyone or anything just to advance their cause," added Demus.

"Demus when Louis and Schmeling fought a second time, I know Louis won, but… what, whatever happened to the German?" I inquired.

"Oh, that fight was in… a… '38 at Yankee Stadium. It was a terrible fight for Schmeling. He lost big – real big. In the 1st round Louis walloped him, with such force that his spine was broken; in not one, but *two* places," answered Demus.

"Oh, ah well," I gasped, "did he live or was he crippled or anything?" I added, still gasping at the thought.

"No, no Suse, that German was tough! He lived to fight again, but not against Louis," replied Demus.

"Why were Americans so much against Schmeling, in '32?" I questioned.

"You see Suse, its all politics. The kidnapping took place in March of '31 and Schmeling fought in April of '32. Here, I'll tell you what happened. Under the cover-of-night, the accused kidnapper, who they say was an immigrant carpenter or some man, used a ladder to climb up to the mansion's second floor nursery," recounted Demus.

"Don't tell me," I interrupted. "Let me guess - the accused was German?"

"You got it!" Exclaimed Demus.

Um,um,um," I said, shaking my head in dismay.

"The nurse had not too long stepped into the hall, thereby leaving the baby alone, but sound asleep. The kidnapper saw his chance – and took it. He left a ransom note asking for a large sum of money," recalled Demus.

"How much?" I questioned, anxiously.

"If this note was paid, he vowed to return the baby, safe and sound. I'm not too sure what happened in between. But, unfortunately in May of '32 the dead body of this innocent baby was found. He's skull had been broken. And to think, the father had forked out the $50,000.00 for his baby, alive. The police never found any fingerprints," added Demus.

"Then how could they have arrested that German immigrant?" I asked, in protest.

"Beats me, just because, just be…" Demus started to say.

"Oh, Demus, spit it out! I know, I know," I interrupted, "just because he was German. The anti-sentiment of the day."

"Suse, didn't Cousin Sophie buy another radio?" Demus asked.

"What would she be doing with two?" I questioned.

"I heard that she donated the first radio to our New Road School," replied Demus.

"That was awfully nice of her, always thinking of others. She hardly had time enough to relax. But she tried to squeeze in time to listen to the matches and hear regular broadcasts," I noted.

As if deep in thought Demus recounted, "Suse, Um, now, I got it!" He shouted, loudly.

"Got what?" I questioned, somewhat startled. He was throwing me off my train of thought.

"It took place in '35… the trial of that Lindbergh baby," added a relieved Demus.

"Do you remember the name of the fella they say was responsible?" I asked.

"They called it the 'Trial of the Century'! The man stood trial – but I don't believe he did it, either. His name... was Bruno Hauptmann," answered Demus.

"Hm, hm, wasn't that something. After the Louis' win of '38, I heard that the white folk put a beating and any black folk they happened to meet. They ran after them, too. It's disgraceful to bother people for no good reason. That happened right here in Nova Scotia, too," I said. "All over North America."

"Suse, that same year our favourite radio station joined with the CBC," stated Demus.

"Demus that's not such a big deal – everybody knows that," I remarked. They're chatting about it enough."

"Maybe so, but Suse, were you aware that Cousin Sophie and... ," I interrupted Demus' question.

"Okay, tell me something, what does the CBC have to do with Cousin Sophie?" I asked, in frustration.

"If you let me explain, maybe I'll be polite enough to tell ya'," commented Demus.

"I'm sorry dear, I get so excited sometimes – finish your story, dear, " I said, apologetically.

"No problem, now where was I? Right, Cousin Sophie. Cousin Sophie said that she and anyone else owing a radio had to pay a two dollar licensing fee, but not for long," reported Demus.

"Wasn't that the time that Jesse Owens, the black runner from America embarrassed Hitler at the Berlin Olympics," I said.

"Hitler, that old thing!" Exclaimed Demus with contempt.

"Jesse Owens didn't embarrass anyone. Hitler embarrassed himself, yes he did. The radio said that he went around taking the citizenship away

from the Jews and acting the fool by ordered his henchmen to smash store windows belonging to Jews," complained Demus.

"Dear you... you *are* going off the subject", I corrected, lovingly.

"Sorry honey, but I can't stand or understand his ideas on folks who are not, as he put it, 'Aryan'. Whatever that means. If, the truth be told, when Owens won the fourth gold medal, Hitler couldn't take it any longer and stormed out of the stadium. He didn't even have the decency to present the medals. Hm, he didn't have any decency at all, but that's beside the point. That same stadium was built to show the world the strength, speed and whiteness of 'Aryan Supremacy', whatever that means," said Demus, mockingly. "

What a fool! What a fool!" he added.

"Well, apparently, the world is just as big a fool as Hitler," I said.

"One black man with four gold medals is not enough to change the minds of men," I quipped, rather emphatically.

"I guess change has got to come in generations. Kinda' like in the Bible when the Israelites wandered around the wilderness for forty years; on account of their unbelief. It wasn't until the older generation had past away, that the youth entered into Canaan Land," said Demus.

"It looks like were gonna have to wait awhile for that dear, perhaps, even a couple of generations," I remarked.

It was a period of time when an ineradictable prejudice controlled the mindset of society. A mindset that time alone could and would heal.

"By the way, wasn't it Charles Lindbergh who flew across the Atlantic? I believe he was the same Lindbergh whose baby was kidnapped and murdered. I'm sure that it was him," said Demus.

"You probably right," I added.

"If it's him, then he and his wife were in the Maritimes about a year after the death of their baby," recalled Demus.

"How's that?" I inquired.

"Perhaps they needed to get away. I heard that their plane landed, here in Eastern Passage before journeying to Newfoundland," recalled Demus.

"Hm, interesting," I said. "I didn't know all that!"

"Demus, I miss Annie Johnson's company, some bad," I admitted.

"Suse, you see her at church activities, don't?"

"Yes, we meet at the Ladies Auxillary, Helping Hand Society and the True Blue Club," I replied. "By the way, Annie started up the True Blue Club, you know," I reported, proudly.

"You don't say!" exclaimed Demus.

"We got busy with our families, now were thankful just to meet at all." I stated. "But it's… it's just not the same. It's not the same."

By now, most of the Smith children had left home to start their own lives. Mom Suse and Papa Demus found something missing in their lives. They realized that the empty-nest syndrome left them wanting. For that reason, as well as the fact that they could always use the extra income, the Smith's had decided to take in boarders.

When it came time to choose the boarders, both Mom Suse and Papa Demus agreed that they would have to be screened. This proved to be a very prudent requirement. Through her keen mind, Mom Suse assessed that the best tenants would be the schoolteachers at their one-room, New Road schoolhouse. The grade level ended at seven or eight, the highest allotted.

A few of the boarders became lifelong friends such as, Mrs. Cromwell, and the Ash family consisting of Buster, Gwen with their children, Wayne and Beverly. The Ash children and Mom Suse's grandchildren soon became good friends. They went to school together and shared many youthful pastimes.

Buster was a hard working truck driver and his wife was devoted to her pupils. She taught several of Mom Suse's grandchildren and family members. The close-knit family fostered a great deal of love and respect in the Smith's family house. Incidentally, these boarders remained at the house for years and became the Smiths' extended family. Once again, the home was filled with a vibrant and infectious atmosphere. The children and their parents loved Mom Suse. At times, she would entertain them with her stories and games. And of course, the families would always look forward to her home cooked meals.

"Well, Mrs. Cromwell, how are you feeling this morning?" I asked.

Mrs. Cromwell sighed and rubbed her eyes.

"I spent all night and into the wee hours of the morning marking papers. A schoolteacher's life isn't really her own. Not that I don't love all of my students, even though, sometimes, they really test my patience," said the teacher.

"I guess it's all in a day's work, isn't it dear? I feel the same way about my life too. If we love what we're doing, it's the only thing that keeps us going, don't you think?" I asked, although I knew the answer.

"That says it all, Mrs. Smith. That says it all," repeated Mrs. Cromwell.

All the children in the neighbourhood used to love playing in the old plum trees that lined the Smiths' backyard. Whenever Mom Suse caught them up in the branches, she'd be sure to chase them out. The children from the community would run to their respective houses while her grandchildren and the Ash children would troop home and be given a list of chores to do. This would teach them a lesson for climbing up the very trees that helped the Smith's earn a living.

As usual, Mom Suse busied herself in the kitchen, and heard the laughter of children in the backyard. But, when it was accompanied with the rustling of branches that could only single out one thing. Mom Suse ran outside to spot the culprits and prepare, once again, to reprimand them for climbing up her trees.

"Okay you fellas," I said, while starring up into the leafy branches to see who was hiding there.

"I want you children to climb down from there, now. And I mean right now!"

Out of the trees came three reluctant, solemn-faced souls. They knew that their frolicking had to come to an end. The first grandchild to appear was Dennis Provo, followed by Rayton Willis.

"Okay Rayton, if you were up in my plum trees, there must be another one of you Willis' hiding up there." I spoke in my 'all-knowing' tone.

Poor Rayton, he knew that it was useless to lie to his grandmother.

Just as the befuddled Rayton was about to speak up for his sister, a tiny voice echoed down through the trees.

"It's just me Granny. It's Vivian," the little girl confessed.

"Well you come down here right away, Vivian Willis." I spoke with as much authority as I could muster, "or I'll come right up there to get you."

"I'll be right down." Vivian called out as she hurried down to face her annoyed grandmother.

"So you thought you could fool your old Granny by staying up in the branches, did you?" I asked.

"Oh no Granny Suse, I couldn't climb down right away because I was eating one of your juicy plums. I'm too small to do two things at the same time," explained Vivian in childhood innocence.

Her grandmother's expression softened.

"But not too small to climb up my trees, are you?" I added.

One could almost visualize the tantalizing and delicious-looking fruit trees that decorated Mom Suse's little plum orchard. Just imagine catching a sent of that sweet aroma that wafted in the summer breeze.

"Okay dear, help me clean up the house a little and then, maybe, just maybe, I'll forgive you." I added as I fixed my attention to the other two offenders. I forced a pretending stern facial gesture.

"As for you two, see that wood over there?" I pointed to a number of freshly chopped chords of wood that lay on the ground.

"I want you to take it and pile it up against the side of the house, and be quick about it," I ordered.

Upon hearing the command, the boys immediately ran over to the woodpile to start collecting the logs. It was highly important for Mom Suse to teach her family that no one lives in an exculpatory state. No, not one; we all have our failures, our ups and downs, including ole granny, herself.

Mom Suse's grandchildren loved her, even when they found themselves in trouble. They had come to appreciate the fact that her discipline was always tempered with kindness.

"I'm sure glad God gave me such a fine family," I said, to Demus, often enough.

"They're a real blessing to us. I don't know how we'd manage without them."

Chapter 10

Due to the ravages of Diabetes, Papa Demus was no longer able to read the newspaper for extended periods of time. Hence, Mom Suse read to him or they spent time taking strolls down 'memory lane'.

"Demus you and I both know that the Indians taught the early French pioneers about Maple Syrup Agriculture and more. Grandmother Annie taught me a lot about the traditional native herbal medicine. There are some Native medicines that are said to cure diabetes that would work along with your insulin injections. But you won't keep your hand out of the sugar bowl and cookie jar long enough for them to work," I said, in gentle rebuke.

"Suse, I only take one or two," said Demus, defensively.

"Yes sir, now ask me if, I believe you? Demus that fibbing has got to stop!"

"I'm doing my best to help you, now ask the Good Lord for strength to help yourself!" I exclaimed.

For a long while, Demus remained silent. He held a pensive thought.

"In the Olympics, at turn of the century, I recall vaguely that a Montreal policeman won Canada's first medal. But, I can't remember the name of the athlete or sport. Um, um, um," I said.

"Say Suse, what are you are thinking on now?" Demus asked.

"Still, it's long after they got rid of the French, here, in Nova Scotia, and they're not, yet accepted. We blacks and Indians have got some lot of company," I said.

"That right! And it's not because we like misery, either," quipped Demus.

"When I work over at the Drug Store in Halifax, I greet a number of people. You know, all of the pain, joy or agony can be seen in the eyes. Uh hm, a few of the European immigrants have told me that their names were changed into English-sounding names. Um hm, said that, if the children are heard speaking their own language in school or … well, well I tell you it's a sad state of affairs," I commented.

This type of negative environment, promoted added dimensions of segregation. On a positive note, societies' attitude has caused these 'marked' people to form connected communities and thereby, retain their culture.

"Demus, remember Thomas Longboat, the Indian runner from Ontario? I believe that he broke the colour barrier. Society thinks that Indians can't do anything, but they sure were doing a whole more for themselves, before the whites came. Yes, and many years before that. Well, Longboat was a smart man." I stated, proudly.

"How's that?" Demus questioned, finally coming out of his fog.

"Glad to see you're still awake, it's not too good to talk to myself, and it doesn't look good either," I said with grin.

"C'mon little lady, answer my question, please and thank you," requested Demus.

"I believe he trained himself and wrote up his own contract. That's what I call, a self-made man!" I exclaimed.

"My grandmammy told mama that to be a chief is not just a cowboy and Indian play thing… it's a serious responsibility. It's the management of an entire band, of course, along with the elders' input. Now, what if the shoe was on the other foot?" I questioned.

"How's that? What exactly do you mean, Suse? Demus asked.

"What if the Indians had gone over to Great Britain or to some place in Europe to invade their land and kill-off their people? Or, how about relocating the British folk on to reserves way out on the moors or in the forests. I am sure that they wouldn't like the sound of that, not one bit. But, for my people this has been all too real.

Not to mention the Shubenacadie Indian Residential School, where you and I know that all manner of evil continues to be inflicted upon our innocent children. And why? To brainwash them into self hate. Um, um, um, and the demons… well, they *all* come out at night," I added, tearfully.

"Suse, my eyes are not so bad that I can not feel your despair. I'm so sorry that this cruel world gave you two crosses to bear: a black woman and, a Native. Oh Lord, how I wish that I could lift them for you. Come over here and sit down beside me. Let me wipe away your tears, my little Indian princess," said Demus, lovingly.

"I, I think it's time that we change the subject Suse, don't you?

"I was just thinking the other day of one of our most beautiful birds, the Canadian Loon. What colour do they turn year-around dear?" Demus inquired.

I was still in the process of composing myself.

"Um, let me see. Well, you know that all birds have to molt or loose their feathers. At that time they are in no shape to fly. In winter their plumage is completely gray, the molting season. In summer they are black and gray with bold spots and highlights of white. They can't walk very well, but they sure can dive - far and fast," I replied.

"One time in a magazine, I recall seeing red throated loons," added Demus.

"I don't think that we have them around here; probably up north. They are the tiniest of the species." I quickly informed him.

"I enjoy listening to their cries. It's as if they are speaking to all creation," commented Demus.

"They probably are. When I was a young girl back home, we would often find ourselves close to the banks of the lake. The loons congregated in the midst of the waters that seemed to glisten like silver. Sure seemed to me, that their sounds proclaim His undisturbed glory," I added.

"Suse, now tell me something, do you remember who bought the first truck in New Road?" Demus asked.

"Sure do, um hm, it was Uncle Will Cain," I answered.

"Wasn't he proud - and some folks said he stole it," I added.

"Yea, fancy a New Road man stealing a truck, driving that distance from town – all without being caught? Not likely, Demus. That's right, Uncle Will worked hard to pay for his truck. He was a labourer from his youth. I'd say he'd earned it," I remarked.

Vivian Willis

"Okay, then who had the first store in New Road?" Demus asked.

"Oh, that's an easy one, why it was old man Fraser, Mr. Isaac Fraser. Um hm, that store was located right next to our St. Thomas Church. The nicest people you ever wanna meet. If a customer didn't have the money, purchases were credited 'til payday. Mr. Fraser never let anyone go without, especially during the Depression years even when his family had hard times," I replied, proudly.

"Tell the truth and shame the devil!" Demus exclaimed.

"And he could stand to be shamed," I added.

"Okay then, did Mr. Bundy tell you who was the proprietor of the Halifax Coun…"

I just couldn't wait, I had to interrupt. "Oh Demus, I surely know *that* answer. It was George Whynder. I heard that Dad's father new him well." I answered, excitedly.

"Suse, I don't see why you, all the time have to rush in. Give a man a chance to finish the question before you answer," said Demus in annoyance.

"Mind ya' honey, it's no harm intended. I'm truly sorry," I confessed in an apologetic tone.

Their was silence for a about minute until Demus came around.

"Say, husband of mine, have you seen the latest styles for women? Oh, it's called the 'military look' with bobby socks. The socks are short, white and turned down. The skirts are shorter too, and they're still wearing crinolines. You know, those lace-layered slips that are starched so stiff, they sometimes scratch the skin. The young girls like the fact that their skirts are wide and colourful. Not to mention, the fashionable two inches of crinoline showing underneath. My, what fashion!" I exclaimed.

"That's fine for everyday wear, but don't play that trick in the House of God. Any man could be mighty distracted. You know what I mean?" I asked.

"Sure do, dear," replied Demus.

"The Good Book asks, "Who can find a virtuous woman?" I quoted.

"Oh, I've found one! Thank you Lord, I found one!" Demus exclaimed, with a grin from ear to ear.

For the most part, when it came to running the household, Mom Suse was a fairly independent woman. Due to her sweet disposition, her house became her grandchildren's the second home. These youths were always waiting to help with a few odds and ends around the house.

"Grandpa Demus, you know you can't have any cookies," said the caring, Vivian.

"You know that if Granny Suse was here, she'd be furious if she knew what you were up to."

"I only wanted one," replied the chastised grandfather. "They smell so good, I couldn't resist."

"You know they're not good for you, Grandpa, besides we want you to live for a long, long time," said Vivian as she put her little arms around the old man's neck. She gave him a big hug. "So please put them back," she added, softly.

"Since you put it that way, my dear, I'll put them back. I wouldn't want your Granny to think that I let her down, would I?" Papa Demus asked.

"Vivian, Vivian!" Mom Suse called from the kitchen. "Will you please go outside and help Genevieve bring in the laundry?"

"Yes Granny Suse," said Vivian. At the time Vivian went outside, a grandson came strolling into the house.

"Hi Granny Suse. I can smell that fresh baking of yours all the way outside. I sure would like to have at least one," said Dennis, while he eyed the platter of cookies.

"Not before dinner," came the reply.

"If you need something to do, why don't you go to the barn and feed the chickens?" I directed

"I'm on my way," said Dennis, before heading out.

"Barbara, would you mind to set the table after you've finished washing the floor?" I asked.

"I'll get to it as soon as I've finished here," replied Barbara.

"That's fine dear. You children are worth your weight in gold. I don't know what I'd to without you," I commented, gratefully.

With so much work to be done during the day, dinnertime was the one time where everybody could get together to discuss the day's activities.

"And how were your classes today children?" I inquired

"We learned the times table today," said Vivian, proudly. "I can count up to ten times ten."

"That sounds interesting dear. I'm sure it will come in handy, later on in life. I hope you continue to pay attention to the teacher," I added, deliberately.

"Oh yes Granny. We've already had a test on it and I only missed one question," said Vivian.

"Well, keep up the good work," I encouraged. "And what about you my dear?" I turned to Dennis who was usually silent during the meals. "What did you learn today? I asked"

"They taught us how to tighten up loose chairs in Shop Class," replied Dennis, sheepishly.

"That doesn't sound like much fun," I admitted.

"It wasn't. I sat on one after I fixed it, and it collapsed right under me," complained Dennis, quite embarrassed.

His cousins all burst out laughing until I gave them one of my you-know-better glances.

"If the shoe was on the other foot, you wouldn't want Dennis laughing at you... would you, now?" I asked.

They hung their little heads in shame.

"Oh dear, I hope you weren't hurt," I stated.

"No, I was sore for awhile though, but at least, I found out what went wrong. I should have let the glue dry longer," added Dennis.

"That's what important my dear," I said softly. "If you learn from your mistakes, you won't repeat them later on. There's an old saying that I learned from my mother. It goes like this, 'You will learn more from your mistakes than your accomplishments'. I hope you fellas remember that."

"We will Granny," chimed the grandchildren.

After dinner, there was still work to do in the Smith household. The granddaughters stayed with Mom Sue in the kitchen. They made jams and applesauce, as well as, the baking for the next day's rounds. Without the help of the younger generation, Mom Suse would have to be up all night, in order to have the items available for sale the next day. When life seemed like, 'two days in one', the industrious Mom Suse never thought of giving up. She always believed that the next day would turn out better. It was this positive mindset that enabled her and Papa Demus to raise their children and grandchildren in the best way possible, on their meager income.

Mom Suse was working in Mr. Mitchell's store and home.

"Well I guess it's time to clean Mr. Mitchell's store," I would whisper to myself after the work was finished in the kitchen.

Mr. Mitchell was so kind that he would often give Mom Suse medicine for her ailing husband.

A regular customer had just entered the store.

"How are you today, Mr. Wilson? I inquired.

"Very well, my dear. And how is your lovely family doing these days?" He asked.

"They're all doing pretty well, thanks to the Good Lord," I replied.

"I heard that your grandchildren have beautiful voices, and that they sing in the choir," commented Mr. Wilson.

"Don't my grandchildren sing like angels," I asked with pride. "My husband and I are so blessed to have such depth of musical talent in our family. We've always played music in our home," I added.

Papa Demus and Mom Suse were, indeed, blessed with musical talent. She extended her skills to her husband. Mom Suse taught Papa Demus his musical notes. Yet, his wife received no formal musical training. Due to his wife's teaching, Papa Demus became the chief organist at St Thomas Baptist Church for over fifty years.

"My, it was a beautiful sermon last Sunday, wasn't it?" Mr. Wilson asked.

"I found it very inspiring. I've been a member of the church all my life. The Lord is my Shepherd and I'll always follow him," I said, in heartfelt conviction.

"It pays to lead a good, clean life doesn't it Mom Suse?" agreed Mr. Mitchell, as he tended to a customer.

"It sure does. Store up the riches in Heaven and let the good Lord to the rest; that's what I always say," I added.

"You certainly have a beautiful way of phrasing your thoughts Mom Suse," commented Mr. Wilson.

"The good Lord puts the words in my mouth, Mr. Mitchell, and all I do is say them."

Humility prevented her from taking any credit.

"Oh, by the way, remind me to bring out some clothes that I have been saving for your grandchildren," said Mr. Wilson.

"It's very nice of you to think of them. I know they will be grateful," I said.

"I know what it's like to come from a big family," noted Mr. Mitchell.

"Your kindness is always appreciated," I replied.

"I do what I can. I know if the shoe was on the other foot, you'd be bringing me bags of clothes," added Mr. Wilson.

When community folks received clothing and food items from Mom Suse, whether second-hand, her handmade creations or famous pastries, it was like attending a rummage sale and getting everything for free.

CHAPTER 11

MOM SUSE'S CALM AND cool nature reflected itself in her manner of handing grave situations. One perfect example was the crises facing Canada during World War II (1939-1945). Citizens had to be on the alert during those six years. The fear of a possible Nazi invasion was real, specifically for Canadians living on the East Coast. This area would have most likely been attacked, first since Halifax was built as a military and naval base. The magnificent star-shaped hilled fortress of Citadel Hill would have been especially visible.

Pauline had not too long passed by her parents' house to assist in her Dad's care. The Air Raid Warden, Mr. Allan Johnston, could be seen approaching the house. His large, white unmarked helmet was highly noticeable. It was strapped under his chin.

"Allan Johnston is coming this way, Mama. I think it's important. Please hurry!" said Pauline, urgently. Her mother was hanging up laundry in the back. In her calm manner, Mom Suse waited until she hung up the last sheet; before walking to the front of the house to greet him.

"Hello Allan," she said as she opened the door. "What seems to be the problem, son?"

"Another Air Raid warning, Mrs. Smith!" Shouted Allan, in near panic.

"You'll have to hurry out into the fields. They say it's a 'national emergency'!"

"Calm down, my boy." My tone was reassuring. "We'll be out in a minute. We have everything ready; food, blankets, ***everything.***"

Vivian Willis

That's good Mrs. Smith, but please... hurry. They say every second counts. Allan didn't realize that Mom Suse had been through this all before.

She had seen the same, desperate behaviour thirty years earlier, during the First World War. After all of her years of living, she accumulated a vast experience in handling tragedies. These trials had given her much insight into the human spirit.

Allan recalled, "Remember the last Air Raid when a group of your grandchildren found themselves in the St. Thomas Church Cemetery? We can't have a repeat...."

"Now, Allan," I interrupted. "How do any of us know where we will be when these warnings are sounded? Come on now! At least they were sensible enough to remain out of sight. Even if I didn't know where they were," I corrected.

The following is an account of what had previously taken place to annoy the warden. Allan Johnston was passing by the cemetery, making his rounds. He thought that he heard children's voices, but he wasn't too sure. Suddenly, their voices were raised in laughter and conversation. Allan walked closer to investigate.

The little group was more startled at seeing Allan Johnston, then at being found in the cemetery. They had wandered off without telling their granny. And they had deliberating ignored the warning signal. The Air Warden advised the guilt-ridden children to hush up quick and stay put until he told them otherwise. And he wasn't the least bit impressed with the fact that their granny had no idea where they were.

Mom Suse realized that they had been given a shock that frightened them near to death. A real disciplinarian, herself, Mom Suse decided that they had been through enough. She was grateful that they were all safe and sound.

"Come on children," I said calmly. Let's get these things outside and wait until Allan returns to tell us it's safe to go back inside."

"Do you really think everything will be alright Mama?" Pauline asked, nervously.

"No, thinking about it," I said in a matter of fact tone. "I know everything will be alright. Just trust in God to protect us from all evil.

Pauline was already feeling much better had kissed her mother on the cheek, and began to gather the supplies they needed to take out in the field. Sure enough, just as Mom Sue predicted, nothing did happen; but it was one more example why Mom Suse became a valued member of the community. Her reputation as a wise woman was deeply rooted in an intimate relationship with God.

During the war years, the City of Halifax and the Town of Dartmouth also experienced what was coined as "Black Outs". Where, in the evening and night hours, all forms of electricity and lighting including kerosene lamps and the like were turned off. Residents were counselled to close their curtains and doors to avoid becoming targets of night attacks.

Finally, the end of the Second World War brought prosperity to Canada including Nova Scotia. Mom Suse had found it easier to make a living selling her goods, due to this economic upswing.

Meanwhile, Mom Suse's dad, Mr. Bundy was in failing health. His mobility was enhanced with the aid of a cane, although his mental acuity remained intact. At this time he was in his nineties. In the black community the old folks were highly respected, and Mr. Bundy was one blest man. He still had his trusty battery-operated radio. Whenever Mom Suse same to visit, it was always a happy occasion. She would forever be his 'little Suse'.

As Mr. Bundy sat in the parlour on his comfortable chair, he reminisced about the old days.

"In the 1930's the provincial government established the Mother's Allowance to provide for widows with two or more children," said Dad.

"I guess at the rate that Demus is going, I may soon need that help myself," I commented, sadly.

"Honey, your future is in the hands of the living God not in the failing health of your husband. Girl, don't you be inviting the angel of death, too soon, now. I don't want to see you worrying for no reason," encouraged Dad.

Mom Suse patted his hands and kissed his bristled, salt and pepper cheek.

"Hm, hm, I remember that at the turn of the century, black railroad porters finally received their due – a wage of $80.00 a month." Dad reported.

"Um yea, but didn't they have to sleep and eat in separate quarters from white folk?" I asked.

"Ya' know that," exclaimed Dad.

"Dad do you recall the name for bogus remedies? Are they what we used to call nostrums?" I asked.

"Girl, you sure right!" Dad replied.

"Did you ever have a need to try any of them?" I questioned.

"No siree! Honey your mother made me enough Indian bush medicine to last a lifetime. So I never had any need for the white man's concoctions," he answered.

"How did people get away with passing off junk in place of medicine?" I asked, somewhat exasperated.

"Little Suse, in the old days, the medical society was not quite as informed. They weren't established enough, to deal with the 'early 'cures'. Besides, the Canadian prisons were just about full to overflowing, and costing the government a fortune. Now, look at Rockhead Prison over there in Halifax? It's a mess… it's too old, too damp, too run down and too full of prisoners." Dad answered.

"Ah, Dad, I don't quite understand what Rockhead Prison had to do with this subject." I commented. But Dad was too busy daydreaming.

"Hm okay, well what… what about Bromo Seltzer? It was always a good product. How much did it cost back then?" I asked.

He finally refocused.

"Ah well, they sold different size bottles, but I remember the cost was 50¢ for a half size or $1.00 for a double," answered Dad.

" I heard tell that the fella who started up the Fuller Brush Company was Nova Scotian. Is that true?" I quizzed.

"Um, I believe that Fuller Brush was in business before the turn of the century, but I can't say. I don't know for sure whether it's a Scotian outfit or not." He replied.

"Dad I'm going to start supper, but before I do, I can say that 1921 was a great year for Canadians when Doctors Banting & Best discovered insulin; medicine to control diabetes. I remember that year clearly, because that's when The Home for Coloured Children opened. Didn't they win the Noble Peace Prize a few years later? If they didn't, then they should have," I quipped before exiting the parlour.

Dad reached over to switch on his trusty battery-operated radio.

"Girl, if you ask me what happened yesterday or last month. I'd be hard pressed to remember. Instead, ask me, what took place in the past, 'cause my mind soaked it all up like a sponge." Dad concluded with a grin.

Although her grandchildren spent many happy hours in their grandparent's home, it was not all fun and games. As mentioned earlier, Mom Suse insisted on teaching them a sense of responsibility in assigning each of them various chores. There was, however, one chore which they were more than obliged to do; that was picking blueberries at the back of the farmhouse on the Smith's large acreage. They would eagerly collect their baskets and await her instructions to begin picking. Every anxious moment was in anticipation of the delicious task at hand.

"Okay children, it's time to collect berries for your grandmother's pies. And I don't want you to eat too many of the berries, this time," I'd often warn them.

"I need them for my customers, not to mention the delicious blueberry pie we'll be having for dinner tonight," I directed.

With visions of tasty desserts dancing in their heads, the grandchildren collected their baskets and ran off into the woods.

"We're gonna have pie tonight!" Young Vivian yelled, unable to contain herself as she ran towards the blueberry patch."

"I'm going to fill my basket first and get two slices for dessert," hollered Dennis, gleefully.

"Not if I collect them first," countered Barbara. The race was on.

Once in the fields, the berry packing began in earnest. The children broke out in joyful singing of "Frere Jacques". The girls began to sing in rounds when the boys joined in. It was followed by, "Billy Boy" until the baskets were near full. The sweet sound of children's voices filled the air making their happy time pass without

Vivian Willis

notice. Within a half-hour, Dennis had been true to his word, and was the first to fill up his basket. He ran at top speed towards the farmhouse and burst through the backdoor.

"I'm back Granny Suse." Dennis spoke with pride as he entered the kitchen. I smiled at his exuberance and patted his thick curly mop of hair.

"I knew that you'd be the first one back, my boy, and all I had to mention was your favourite dessert. Well, any boy who is such a hard worker deserves an extra big slice tonight. Why don't you try and fill up another basket. The more berries I have to work with, the more I'll be able to make," I encouraged.

"May I have another basket, please?" Implored Dennis. "I'll fill it up *higher* that the last."

"I'll hold you to that dear," I said, still smiling.

Mom Suse bent down under the sink and pulled out another basket. As she handed it to him, Dennis was already halfway out of the door.

"I'll be back in no time because I'm the best berry picker in the whole wide world!" Dennis yelled, over his shoulder.

A few minutes later, two more grandchildren walked in with overflowing baskets. Mom Suse hauled the baskets to the sink; after washing them, she asked, "Did you have fun girls?"

"It sure was fun Granny," replied Vivian.

"I can see by the big, blue smiles on your faces that you fellas had a lot of fun. Why don't you help your old Granny wash these berries so I can get them ready for the pies? Maybe add a pot of blueberry duff with loads of fat dumplings... fluffy as clouds. Then, later on, you can help me make the blueberry jam for our tomorrow's toast," I suggested.

The children nodded their heads. It was a special treat to help their grandmother in the kitchen. "Okay children, let's get started. Dennis and Genevieve will be back soon with the rest of the berries." As soon as she spoke, the youngest grandchild came in with her basket.

"I'm sorry, it took me so long to pick these Granny." Genevieve's voice was close to breaking as she watched her sisters busy at the sink. "I tried to be fast, really I did."

"It doesn't matter how fast you are dear," I said kindly. It matters only, that you do the best possible job and nothing else matters."

A smile crossed the child's face as she joined her sisters. The kitchen work was well underway when Dennis returned with his second load of berries.

"Glad to see you dear. Once you've put your basket in the sink, why not you go out to feed the chickens and pigs. They're probably as hungry as you," I commented.

She could see by the way he walked that he was tired and sore from the backbreaking task of berry picking. Her expression softened.

"But before you do that why don't you relax with a tall, cool glass of lemonade and a peanut butter sandwich?"

"That sounds great Granny," answered Dennis.

Being very astute and fair-minded, Mom was not one to treat any child different from the rest. She extended the offer to one and all, and naturally, all accepted. By the time evening had darkened the horizon, dinner was ready and the table was set. Amid the tantalizing aroma, the children all spoke about the day's activities. When the food arrived, silence descended and the children were ever mindful of the anticipated dessert. They 'cleaned their plates'. After everyone had enjoyed two slices of pie, the girls went into the kitchen to help their grandmother with the dishes.

Dennis was instructed to keep an eye on his grandfather. Papa Demus had a real sweet tooth when it came to sugar cubes that could spell disaster for his diabetes-ravaged body. Dennis reached the dining room, just in the nick of time. Grandfather Demus was holding a cube of sugar to his mouth. He was caught in the act.

"Grandpa, put that down, immediately", directed young Dennis as he waggled his finger in front of his grandfather's face. "You know you aren't supposed to have any sweets. Granny says it's bad for your health."

Dennis removed the offending sugar cube from Papa Demus' hand and returned it to the bowl. His tone lightened as he went over to hug the elderly man.

"We all love you grandpa, and want you to be around forever. So-o please, please stay away from the sugar," pleaded Dennis.

"I'll try my boy. All I've been able to smell today are those pies and that pot of blueberry duff, and I guess I wasn't thinking. You march into the kitchen and tell your granny that I am sorry," said a remorseful Papa Demus.

Upon entering the kitchen, Dennis promptly reported the news to his me. "Granny… and I *was* able to take the cube away before he ate it, just in the nick of time!" The vigilant boy spoke with pride.

"That's a good boy, Dennis," I replied. "I know that I can rely on you children to help me out. Now how would you like another small piece of pie? She didn't have to ask twice. By the time she had the slice of pie on a plate, Dennis was seated at the table. Between mouthfuls, he declared.

"You sure do make the best pie in town Granny, probably in the whole wide world."

"I don't know about the whole world Dennis dear," I said. "But I believe that I make a mighty fine pie," I added.

The next morning, Mom Suse received much comments of praise from her grandchildren for her freshly prepared blueberry jam as they heaped spoonfuls on their toast. Mom Suse took the compliments in stride but warned them.

"Children, I don't want you overdoing it. I don't want any of you to get a sore stomach from eating too quickly," she added.

"Don't worry Granny," said Dennis between mouthfuls of toast.

"We wouldn't think of it." Vivian added. "I could eat twice as much of your cooking and not get sick." Then noticing her grandmother's bemused expression, Vivian added, "But we'll all be careful."

Ironically, a few hours later, it was Vivian who had retuned with a paled complexion, while complaining of a stomachache.

"Now what did I say at breakfast?" I asked and couldn't help but let out a little chuckle.

"No matter though, I'll just give you a taste of cherry bark tea and you'll be feeling right as rain," I concluded.

Mom Suse knew exactly what home remedy was needed for which occasion, and by mid-afternoon, Vivian was romping around outside as if the cramps never happened.

CHAPTER 12

"**H**ALLELUJAH, NO MORE AIR raids! Sure glad the war is over, Demus. Thank God from whom all blessings flow! I exclaimed. Things seem to be picking up for us now, and I know it's easier on your mind too," I commented in relieved.

"Hey, Demus, I heard on the radio that when Halifax's Pier 21 opened after the Great War, thousands and thousands of war brides and British children arrived on Scotian shores."

"Suse that's good and dandy, but what does Canada say about the almost one thousand Jewish refugees from Nazi Germany? And who turned them away?" Demus asked totally exasperated.

"Ah, shame, shame, but it seemed as though Canada acted like a Nazi supporter. Yea, so did Cuba, America and near five other countries down south, there," I replied in an irate tone.

"Can you imagine yourself as a Jewish refugee on this ship crammed with hundreds of people, who have been sailing for days on end?" Demus inquired. "Only to be rejected at every port simply because…"

"Because of the anti-Jewish sentiment," I finished.

"What happened to the Golden Rule? 'Do unto others as you would have them do unto you'." Demus quoted.

"Oh Demus, that's just for show. When the chips are down, make-believe Christians show their true colours. That's it ya' know!" I exclaimed.

"What's it?" Demus asked.

"The manner in which we Christians care for the lowly. It shows how much we love Jesus. To go out of our way to help a stranger, that's love. There is no true love without sacrificing – without going that extra mile," I added.

"Tell me, Suse was it in the '20's that the government turned the French Fortress in Cape Breton into an Historic Site?" Demus inquired.

"You mean the Louisburg Fortress? Is that the fort that was destroyed by the British when the French were thrown out of the province? Talk about smoothing over your conscience," I commented.

"You know Suse, we have lived through two world wars and the effects of both have been far-reaching," Demus said, pensively.

"Yea, far-reaching into our pocket-book, too," I stated while sipping on a cup of cocoa.

"There was a ration on almost everything," I added.

"The gas ration was what? I believe 40 mph. to save on fuel." Demus recalled.

"And don't forget the butter ration. Thank God we had our own faithful cows and chickens to provide for our dairy needs." I reported.

"Remember the tires honey, there was a ration on those too." Demus commented.

"What on earth for?" I questioned.

"After the Japanese bombed Pearl Harbour, the area wasn't safe anymore. That was around the same area where rubber was produced," answered Demus.

"Oh, I didn't know all that," I said.

"Hm, but I do know that liquor is the drink of the devil. It turns people into demons," I said. "Seems like ever sense our men and women returned from overseas, the celebrating and carrying-on is… is pretty near, hellish. Why, everybody's heard about the streetcar that our servicemen set fire to on Barrington Street. It was right around VE Day," I added.

VE Day (Victory in Europe), took place on May 7th and 8th of 1945. The dates signify when the Germans surrendered to the Allies.

"Now, when did **vandalism** become a new word for celebration?" I asked.

"Speaking of the devil, what to say about the way in which that *fool* and his wife themselves in?" Demus asked.

"Demus, who are you calling a *fool*? It has to be Hitler. No one else but Hitler, isn't it?" I asked, chuckling to myself.

"Um, Hitler, that *old* thing and his *fool* wife Eva," answered Demus.

"They committed suicide, together. I believe that he took a cyanide tablet first, and then gave one to her. On top of that, he decided to shoot himself to make sure the job was done right," recalled Demus.

"Um, um, you were right Demus, they lived as fools and so they died as fools," I commented.

"See, those fools took the easy way out. They were complete cowards, especially Hitler. He wanted to avoid a trial and an execution. He disgraced himself," said Demus, emphatically.

"That's his legacy… a disgrace. Um, um, um, those fools didn't know that everyone must meet their Maker. There is no short-cut to heaven, but I guess there's one to hell, and that's a scary thought," I added.

"Seems like its time for God to reconstruct some souls around here. That's what they did after the Second World War, ya' know, they reconstructed the cities and towns. Down south and even up here," stated Demus.

"Most likely, they'll be making some changes here sooner than you think," he added.

"Demus, I been kinda thinking – about Halifax," I said.

"You mean that you've been thinking about Africville, don't you? Demus chuckled.

"You're insight is down-right frightening. Suse, are you having another premonition or something? Oh, oh that Indian blood is rising up again. Um, I think I'll leave you alone, in here," joked Demus.

"Demus you stay right here," I teased. "Do you know how the cities in North America rid itself of slum housing? I'll tell ya', by having the firemen deliberately set the buildings on fire. Sometimes house by house," I revealed

"Deliberately? Hm, I guess they can do what they want 'cause they're in charge, but... deliberately"? Demus repeated, almost in disbelief.

"And what about those women who linger around the street corners, attracting the soldiers stationed in town. Um, you can see them sitting in the restaurants, as they enjoy a convivial evening," I said.

"Hm, Suse, tell me something. Why is it that the white folk call street beggars, 'street trash'? They all the time using that word '*trash*'. They even call their own, 'white trash', I just don't understand it." Demus commented, in frustration.

"Oh Demus, you know why, but you do too much pretending. Anyway, Grandpappy Cain told me about the days of American slavery. He said that some white sharecroppers were *so-o* poor that they had to eat out of the trashcans. Yes siree! Grandpappy said that it happened so often, that their own people labelled them 'white trash'. And poor white folk have been scorned ever since," I said, sadly.

"You know Demus, folks don't much like the Irish either. Especially, the black Irish. My grandmammy was Indian and Irish. They scorned her like she was the devil's mistress," I said.

"That's not the real reason. It's probably jealousy, because she was so-o beautiful with her pretty dark complexion, and long, gorgeous hair," added Demus.

"Hm, you so right. So anyway Demus, don't worry about what they call one another because it doesn't affect you, any. Just worry when one of them up and calls us that cursed, 'N' word," I said.

"Suse, now ***don't*** go 'getting my goat'. 'Cause I'm ***too*** old and I'm ***too*** tired," said an agitated Demus.

"They don't have the sense that God gave them," he added.

"Okay dear, I'm sorry," I said, soothingly. "No harm intended."

"They've done Africville wrong, all wrong. It's great to build up the cities and things. But, Africville has received nothing but the bad end of the stick. They pay their fair share of taxes just like the rest of Halifax. Instead of providing the residents with the necessary services the city burdens them with, 'services' that they wouldn't think of placing in white communities," I stated.

"Demus, you know something?" I whispered, "Our cities are *really* under siege."

"The war is over – what on earth are you talking about, woman? What are you talking about?" Repeated Demus as he shook his head in annoyance.

"Listen here Demus, the other day I finished working at the drugstore when I ran into a distant relative of mine. He looked so-o bad and scruffy, that I hardly recognize him. I thought that he lived out here. Um um, he said that his underworld life had made him a self-possessed man. Hm yea, he was self-possessed all right. He was possessed with a little too much homebrew," I added.

"Oh, the poor fella's probably waging a personal war with… with," hesitated Demus.

"My, my, Demus go ahead and spit it out… a war with liquor. He's not the first and he won't be the last. God love him, though," I added, sweetly.

"I told you Demus, that our cities are under siege," I reiterated.

"I can't understand what she's talking about," mumbled Demus.

"The war is over now! Suse, the war's been *over*! Repeated Demus.

The last time Mom Suse visited her dad he had continued to take his favourite seat, in the Cherry Brook Baptist Church. Recently, a sharp change had transpired, and his health took a turn for the worse. The doctor said it was his heart – it seemed to be slowing down. Due to his inability to climb stairs so the family moved Mr. Bundy to the bedroom on the main floor.

"Suse, the doctor has been my physician for a mighty long time, but the man's not God. He can't predict exactly when I'm going to depart this old world," declared dear ole Dad. And it wasn't soon after that Dad had passed.

Mr. Bundy had 'finished his earthly fight' and was resting in Jesus. As was the custom, the Wake was held in the family home for two days. The body was placed on a 'cooling board' in the parlour until a coffin was either, hand made or purchased. On the third day, the funeral service was held in the Cherry Brook Baptist Church. It was filled to capacity, and them some. Most of the men stood outside to allow sufficient seating for the women and children. To indicate that a death was recent, men wore black bands on the left upper arm. Those were the days when men also wore hats.

Not long after her dad's passing, Mom Suse was awakened in the middle of the night. She heard the dogs barking. Normally, she would have slept right through their shenanigans, but the grieving process is often accompanied by restlessness.

"Let me see what time it is?" I whispered to myself.

Then I got up to illuminate the kerosene lamp.

"Demus you sleeping honey?" I asked. "Those dogs woke me up and I can't get back to sleep. Demus you sleeping?" I asked, almost pleadingly.

Papa Demus thought that he heard Mom Suse the first time, and believed it to be apart of his dream, until her hand gently pushed his shoulder. It was then that he woke up. Papa Demus yawned for a moment as he shifted on his right side, to face is wife. He adjusted his eyes to the light by blinking and rubbing them with his left hand. He slid his right hand slid under her neck. Mom Suse lay on her left side facing him.

"Dear, thank you for your company. No matter how sleepy and tired you feel, your selfless love has always had energy enough for me," I commented with gratitude.

"Suse, Mr. Bundy just past away a month ago. The grieving process is a natural response to a loss, a great, great loss," commented Demus.

"You know something honey, some time after burying my Dad, I was so overcome with grief. I pretty near ran into the woods… to my favourite spot and I cried like a baby. I'm not ashamed to say it. Mama said that tears are a healing balm," I admitted.

"Demus, how come you all the time, called my father, Mr. Bundy. Of the forty-two years since we've 'jumped the broom', not once have I heard you call my father anything else like, Papa or Dad. Why not?" I quizzed.

"Since I first met your parents we all got along. It is with deepest respect that I called him, 'Mr. Bundy'. Your father understood that and appreciated it. At first, I think he felt a little taken back, but in time he came to understand me. He became my best buddy and a good old friend… full of wisdom and love. Why Mr. Bundy and I, we use to share information from the newspapers and the radio, and anywhere else. I reckon, I have to look entirely to you now, honey," replied a sleepy Demus.

Mom Suse caught Papa Demus dozing off.

"Demus you sleepy yet?" I asked, but wishing that he was wide-awake.

"Girl, once I lay my head down, I'm always ready for sleep. You know that, 'cause your so-o sharp," teased Demus.

"Ya' dear, but I *don't* cut," I replied.

They laughed out loud, almost forgetting about their sleeping boarders. Mom Suse blew out the lamp while Papa Demus got comfortable under the blankets, but apparently not comfortable enough.

"Babe, you move a little closer and warm me up. I'm getting *cold*," he added.

Chapter 13

Mom Suse and her daughter Pauline were again, conversing about the Shubenacadie Indian Residential School. By now, Pauline was a married woman with children of her own. It pretty near tore her heart out to learn of these continued injustices. In times past, Papa Demus and Mom Suse used to attend the Pow wow's at the Shubenacadie and Millbrook bands.

"Can you imagine, Pauline? The authorities snatched the children from their homes! Out of their parents arms!" I exclaimed.

After a long pause, I continued.

"Um, um, um, I suspect, that the parents were as the 'living dead' when the children had gone. Um, hm, innocents are herded away to live in an atmosphere of hate. They are forced to become 'white'. The children learn that their music, song, dance, drums, food and traditions are *not* important. They are forced to dress in white peoples clothes with white people's hairstyles. Um, and the hair is cut so crudely and ugly. Um hm, and these children are forced to speak English, too," I added.

"What if they don't know English, then what? Pauline inquired.

"Well, it's the accepted language... period. The children are punished... often, just for sport. Pauline, the demons come out at night... you know what I mean! I tell you, this school is the devil's work, cruel and malicious," I added.

"Mama, what kind of school *is this*? Questioned Pauline, looking overwhelmed.

"A 'school' where *all* traces of culture is erased," I replied.

"Well, when did this so-called school open, anyway? Was it after the start of the Great Depression. Hm, another thing, why has it been allowed to go on so long?" Asked Pauline, obviously exasperated.

"Ah, honey, it seems that the government and the church have the right to keep it going. This joke of a 'school' opened around 1922. It's no telling when it'll close. Can't be soon enough, if you ask me," I replied.

"Mama, first the white man runs the Indians off *their* land; herds them out to reservations. If that isn't enough, they snatch away their children. Shame, shame, shame! I think that his school is run by *monsters* parading around as people." Pauline said, in anger.

"The government and the church have to 'get their minds right'!

It would start, if they close the school down and return the children home. Wouldn't hurt none, if they realize their wrongs, either," she added.

"Yes, daughter, but by the time many return home, they don't know their parents... or their culture. And, I certainly agree that people must take responsibility for the wrong they do." I remarked. "Especially, if you say that you're acting, on behalf of a church. Um um, what a crying shame! Yes, and I remember something else, Pauline. Many of the students were 'sterilized'. You understand me? They will not be able to have their own children." I commented, as tears welled in my eyes.

Pauline could sense that something else was on my mind.

"Mama, what else is troubling you?" she inquired, softly.

"Well, Pauline, I am reminded of the great indebtedness we have to the Indians of New Road. It was the mid 1800's when the authorities left us in the backwoods with next-to-no provisions. Miraculously, God answered our prayers of sustenance. The God Lord sent us to where the Indians lived. They, in their kind wisdom shared with us; *they* taught us how to survive. So the following spring when the authorities returned 'up home', they brought empty carts. Carts to hold our dead. Just imagine! You see, as the old folks recounted to us, 'we were not expected to last the winter'." I recalled.

"Now, concerning this old school, tell me, Pauline, what can heal a damaged heart?" I asked.

"Mama, we've got to leave *our people*, in the hands of God!" answered Pauline.

"Um hm, some people *know* how to stand up for what *they* believe in. Do you know that Demus?" I asked, emphatically. "The minister told us about the situation on Sunday. He encouraged us to pray for Viola, and the NSAACP. Too bad you weren't there, 'cause that particular morning you were on the 'down and low'.

"Suse, what are you going on about, now!" Demus questioned, in slight frustration.

"Um hm, Viola Desmond made headlines in New Glasgow and beyond. I'll tell you why. She was sitting in the main level of the Roseland Theatre... um hm, refused to go up stairs to the 'Negroe Section'. This was on November 8th, 1946. The police took her right to jail; did you know that, Demus? Um hm, her decision was to either pay a fine of $20.00 or spend thirty days in jail." I reported, proudly.

"That's right, that lady's had a devil of a time. The police jailed her for twelve hours, and charged her with planning to defraud the government," added Demus.

"Oh, so I guess you *know* the story," I said. "And you acting all quizzical," I commented.

"Um, sho' do," replied Demus. The NSAACP or the Nova Scotia Association for the Advancement of Coloured People, came to her rescue and raised funds towards her fine."

"She couldn't afford to spend thirty days in jail for a crime she didn't commit. If you can call refusing to pay one penny, a crime," I concluded.

"This prejudice thing is just one big mess. The white folks brought it in. and I reckon they ain't too eager to take it out," remarked Demus.

"Um, um, um, Demus, did you see the new style swimsuits?" I asked, somewhat perturbed.

"No – wait, yes, yes it has two pieces. It's a little too revealing, though. Looks like she's running around in less than her drawers. Stripping herself of dignity. Shame, shame, women now-a-days have *no* shame!" Exclaimed Demus.

Mom Suse: Matriarch of the Preston area Black Communities

"That's the whole ides, I guess. It's post-war days where a woman has absolutely no self-respect. Oh, the times, they are a changing," I said.

Mom Suse and Papa Demus continue their lively conversation while relaxing, in their bedroom.

"You know what I heard Suse? Down in the States it's illegal now to allow segregation on buses," reported Demus.

"In some ways were worse off up here, than they are down south. Down there, folks admit to being prejudice, but here in Canada, society plays the fool. They make *you* think that *you're* discriminating against them," I said.

"You girl, I hear ya', loud and clear," added Demus.

"Suse before I fall asleep, I've got some good news for ya'. It's about our black community in New Glasgow.

"Go ahead, I'm listening sweetie," I said.

"You heard of Carrie Best?" he asked.

"Oh yes, we met at the Association in New Glasgow," I answered.

The AUBA (African United Baptist Association) of Nova Scotia organizes an annual weekend convention that is hosted (on a rotating basis) by a specific black community. During the convention the visiting members, family and friends from away, are traditionally, billeted in the host community.

"Mrs. Best is the publisher of her own newspaper!" Demus proudly exclaimed.

"You don't say! Oh my, what a smart woman. See, Demus, we black folks have all kinds of sense," I exclaimed.

"Uh hm, if we are given the chance for development, that's the key," he added.

"Dear, that's true in part, but we're still responsible for making our own way in the world. If we women and men folk just stayed in the Preston area, then business would be brisk. But we realize that the big bad world is where the money is," I noted. "Demus, so when we blacks are stung by the foul disposition of the world; and that's *everyday*. It's the reason we grow a second skin.

We black folks make excellent actors, you know. We can change at the turn of a dime!"

Vivian Willis

Mom Suse snapped her fingers and moved her shoulders in unison with each word. "Just like that!"

Demus couldn't help but smile. "Girl, you something else," he said.

"Her newspaper is called 'The Clarion'. She writes about the injustice that we face. Things like not being allowed in certain establishment such as restaurants and segregation in theatres, schools, etc. The good thing is that Mrs. Best, gives hope for the days ahead when our folks will be given equal treatment," reported Demus.

"Amen and Amen!" I exclaimed. Then I paused a moment.

"Demus, you sleepy yet?"

"Not quite babe, what are you thinking on?" he asked.

"Oh no, don't tell me, it's Africville, again."

"The deed says that the community was founded in the mid 1800's, but you and I know that these folks have lived there about a fifty or more years before that," I added.

"Dear, the Bedford Basin area is a real gem. You know how the authorities are always making a big deal about lakefront and waterfront property. That's 'cause it's prime land. The community of Africville is located on prime land. Why else do you think that the government continues to do such nasty things to undermine the land value? Perhaps so that the community would get fed up and move to another location," said Demus.

"Well folks haven't moved out yet with all of the nonsense the city has thrown at them. Are you saying, that they may end up getting kicked out?" Suse inquired.

"I don't know, Suse. I don't know the future, that's your department," Demus answered, with a smile.

"But it seems logical, if we look at the pattern of things," he added.

"Oh, this is so-o distressing," I said and shook my head.

"Honey, you blow out the lamp and bring our sweet self over here, so *we* can get comfortable," added Demus.

This special walk down memory lane was close to home... closest to the heart. Now and again, Mom Sue and Papa Demus would speak about Annie V. Johnson.

"Ah, she sho' was trusted and true. I could tell her anything and not a word would ever get back to me," I recalled.

"That's because Annie was very business-like with people who weren't here friends," commented Demus.

"You sho' right," I agreed.

"You know that some folks called her prissy and stuck up. They even say that the Johnson folks are way, too proud. Well, I tell ya', I'd rather be proud than ashamed," I said, in defence. She was a Beals before marriage, you know," I added. The Beals are proud people... came from Georgia."

"Ah don't pay them chatty fools no mind", said Demus.

"They have nothing to live for and curse anyone who does."

"Ain't that something dear? How Annie suffered a short period of sickness and past away at age 51? I believe, it was a heart condition; she had troubles from birth. It was a difficult month. Annie past away, just days after Viola Desmond's Civil Rights case," I concluded.

"Hm, Demus you know that I don't care much for the sport of baseball, but a black man has just signed on to the league. Now don't ask me which team. But I remember his name. It's Jackie Robinson, an American fella. And may God be with him, 'cause he's sure's gonna need it." I quipped.

"Suse, have you heard anymore about Babe Ruth? Um, he's about as old as I am, slowing down some, too," said Demus.

"Just like we predicted girl, the post-war reconstruction has begun, in earnest, around Halifax. Did you get a chance see to the large Eaton's Building at the corner of Barrington and Prince Streets? It's about four or five stories high and takes up near half the corner lot." Added Demus.

"Nope, can't say I have and can't say that I'm interested," I replied.

"Demus, I got a question for you. In the late 1800's, who do you think was responsible for the first open-heart surgery?" I asked without waiting for a response. A black doctor, yep' an American named Dr. Daniel Williams. I came across an old, brochure while tidying up the drugstore. It said that Dr. Williams had sewn up the first stab wound to the heart." I mentioned, proudly.

"You don't say!" Demus exclaimed.

"Normally they placed the patient in a cool cellar and left them there to die. But Dr. Williams changed all of that foolishness. His open-heart operation was the first of its kind." I added.

"Man, Dr. William must have had to use a lot of laudanum," commented Demus.

"And then some, 'cause if he used too much, the patient would have slept for days," I said.

"Ain't that the truth," said Demus.

"Um, um, um, "I hummed with a pensive expression.

"What you ruminating about?" Demus asked.

"You know how the tides follow the moon's cycle? Why do you think that is?" I quizzed.

"Dear, everything in nature can't be reasoned away. Nature itself is perfectly obedient to the forces of its Creator. The shame rests with human beings, who have turned out to be ungrateful," replied Demus.

"Um, um, um," I said.

"Oh, oh what concerns you now?" Demus asked.

"I believe it happened in the early '20's when Marcus Garvey traveled to Halifax, Sydney and Glace Bay, Cape Breton. Wasn't he was born in Jamaica?

"I can't help you out there, 'cause I don't know anything about Garvey," admitted Demus.

"Well papa told me about him sometime after I gave birth to our Pauline.

"Dad always had a lot of respect for Garvey. Said he was a man of vision, yes siree! Yep, right smart! He planned to have a large gathering of coloured folks from the West Indies, the States and Canada. They were to follow him right back to Africa, to start anew. Where our people would not be treated as second-class citizens," I recalled.

"How come this important information is kept top secret?" Asked Demus.

"It was **never** top secret, Demus. It's just that at the time when Garvey travelled to Nova Scotia, we were busy with Pauline's birth.

Demus, you know that people don't often talk in the pattern of world events. They talk about events sometimes months or years later when, either something or someone jogs their memory. Or the Good Lord brings it mind." I explained, patiently.

"Alright, okay I'm sorry dear, you're right," confessed Demus. "Excuse me honey, maybe I'll go and take a short nap. Don't forget to call me for supper."

"No problem sweetie, you go ahead and lay your burdens down." I said,

Shortly afterwards, Mrs. Ash, one of her boarders entered the kitchen. She apologized to Mom Suse for keeping such a low profile, but was busy completing her personal research on our church history.

"Mrs. Smith, I know that you have to prepare for supper now, but do you think you could oblige me for a moment longer?" Mrs. Ash asked, politely.

"Of course. I'll be much obliged," I said.

"Is it a known-fact, that you're an expert on church history?" Asked the teacher.

"Oh, I wouldn't say I'm an expert, but I can give you a paragraph or two," I confessed.

"Actually, that's all the information that I'll need." Mrs. Ash gratefully replied.

"On a spiritual level, our people always enjoyed serving the Lord. Father Preston 'took the helm'. He was born in 1790, a slave in the tobacco fields of Virginia. He escaped to Nova Scotia in 1816, searching for his mother whom he found in East Preston. She happened to recognize him by a scar on his face. By 1832 African Baptists formed our own religious organization, the AUBA (African United Baptist Association)." I recalled.

"How did the name St. Thomas Church some about?" Asked Mrs. Ash.

"You see, Father James Thomas was a Welshman married to Hannah Saunders of East Preston; were they lived. He was the second preacher after Father Benson Smithers. When Smithers left in 1861, then Father Thomas began his ministry. The 'New Road' church was named, the 2nd Preston, it joined the AUBA in 1856. Later the church was re-named St. Thomas United Baptists in recognition of Rev. Father James Thomas," I recalled.

"Mrs. Ash, you know that the church has always been the cornerstone of our black communities. Our black preachers were either: slaves, freeborn or purchased freedom preachers. It has been written that, "He was born in the house of bondage". "Like many of has co-workers, (he had no) advantage of an early education. *__He depended almost entirely upon the workings of inspiration.__* Some knew what it was like to travel on foot from Yarmouth to Halifax [from the Preston area to Halifax]". In fact, 1939, the Rev. William Perly Oliver spoke on the lack of education as a form of 'mental apartheid'. He added, "Torn as they were from the land of their birth and forced under great cruelty to become a beast of burden, their [only] salvation was in Almighty God," I continued to recite.

"Negro Spirituals is an original form of African North American music. 'In the forests, in the rice-swamps, in the cotton fields, in the cane breaks, behind the stonewall" is where many got their religion'. In the eyes of the slave master, it was a great crime to openly practice religion or to desire the gift of literacy," I proudly recalled.

After receiving the information, the teacher thanked her landlady.

"Miss. Smith you're a life-saver. No… you're a living doll," said an elated Mrs. Ash.

"Um, um, um," I whispered.

"It sure feels good to help someone, it sure feels good."

After supper, Papa Demus and Mom Suse took their usual places in the parlour. It was time for another walk down memory lane.

"Suse, this took place some time after we tied the knot. Your father told me that doctors would prefer their patients to consume beverages made from barley grain instead of coffee. It seemed that the coffee drinkers complained of sluggishness of the heart," recalled Demus.

"Oh, that's not *too* good," I said.

"Demus can you remember what the price of coal was during the Great Depression? I asked.

"Hm, yep sure do. We paid 50¢ to have a bag of coal delivered. Back then, I got a package of tobacco plugs for only 10¢," answered Demus.

Mom Suse: Matriarch of the Preston area Black Communities

"Folks said that they had to stand in 'bread lines' and 'milk lines'. The government gave out oil coupons for kerosene lamps and such. Along with a food coupon resembling a book of stamps. Remember that the only type of fruit a family could only buy were bananas, apples and oranges," I said.

"I even heard tell, that the Indians in Cape Breton, shared their provisions with poor white folk. They helped save their lives. Just like the Indians helped us when we first came to New Road," I added, most proudly.

"Um, um, nothing as good as that bread, is it honey?" Demus asked.

"Man, I don't have a clue what *you're* getting at? Do you want to keep me in suspense?" I joked.

"Okay, I'll share it. The bread I'm talking about has nothing to do with money. Back in the day, the Indians taught our pioneering people how to make bannock bread. Sometimes we call it flour bread, because the recipe is nice and simple. Isn't there a lake by the same name here in Dartmouth?"

"Oh, yes, and the bread *is* filling. It bakes real easy, too" I recalled.

"Some of the old folks are still making moccasins for their family. They sure are comfortable. Remember Suse? I used to make them for us. I'm too old for that now," he added, sadly.

"My those sheep of ours sure came in handy, didn't they?" I asked

"I loved the meat, it was soft and tasty!" Demus recalled.

"No, I'm not thinking on the meat. Don't you remember that we had our homemade remedies?"

"Oh, yes for colds and the flu; the poultice we made from the sheep manure. Well, I tell you once it was made up, none could tell where it came from. And it worked *some* good!" Demus recalled.

"It worked better and faster than the medicine prescribed by the doctor," I agreed.

"Don't you know it?" Exclaimed Demus.

"Demus, sometime ago we were talking about the last boxing match with Joe Louis and Max Schmeling. Wasn't that match in '38. Do you remember that when Louis won that match? Some white

Vivian Willis

folks in Glace Bay took their frustrations to the street - on any black person, in sight. I think that foolishness occurred in Halifax too, but don't quote me on that," I said.

"We better start getting ready for bed. Honey you feeling sleepy yet?" I inquired.

"You bet, I'm so tired, now that I could sleep like baby," replied Demus.

"Um, hm, and snore like a beast... but I still love ya'," I grinned.

As usual, the next day found Mom Suse busy in her kitchen. It was after school when two of her granddaughters, Vivian and Genevieve ran into the house. They told their granny that they had permission to stay for supper.

Before she had a chance to respond, the giggling girls showered her with hugs and kisses.

"Oh Granny Suse, I just love you," said Genevieve.

"Me too," added Vivian.

"Honey babies, I love you both, right back," I said.

'Um, um Granny Suse, I have a question. Do you know what is natural springs or spring waters?" Genevieve asked.

"Now where did you hear something like that at?" I quizzed.

"From the radio today," replied the young granddaughter.

"Honey chile, they are the source of healing waters. Now according to the Indians, they say that the waters can heal the skin and all manner of sickness. Others have said that it cures their rheumatism. You know, when some people get old their bones ache," I said, with a smile.

"Do we have any natural springs up here in New Road?" Vivian asked.

"Not that I know of, although if I remember correctly, there are two in Cape Breton and one in the Valley," I answered.

"Thank you ma'am, it's always good to talk to a grandmother who has all of the answers," said Genevieve.

"No girl, God alone has *all* the answers. I only have some, " I corrected.

"Seems like that's good enough for me!" Genevieve exclaimed.

Mom Suse scurried around her kitchen to prepare the evening meal. Young Vivian and Genevieve sat at the table with tons of unanswered questions spinning around their heads.

"Granny Suse?" Genevieve calls out.

"Did you ever wear a 'hobble skirt'?"

What's a hobble skirt look like, anyway?"

"Where on earth did you hear this?" I questioned.

"Well, the Ladies Auxillary had a meeting at our house a few weeks ago. I heard mama and the ladies talking about clothes that people used to wear. I said to myself, 'hobble', that name sounds like a toy, not a skirt," admitted Genevieve.

"You know girls, that your not suppose to listening in on big people's conversation," I chided.

"Well, I was helping mama carry in the refreshment tray," said Genevieve, in her defence.

I couldn't help but let a chuckle escape.

"Okay, honey chile, my apologies; but that style was in before the '20's, I think, when I was thirty-five years old.

"Oh, Granny Suse, then how old are you now?" Vivian quizzed.

"Hm, let me see? I'm about sixty-four years old, right now," I answered.

"Wow that's a big number, but it's not *that* big. It's not like one hundred or something," sighed the child.

"Okay, the hobble skirts were long and they fit a little close at the hemline," I explained.

"Then how could you get in a car or up on a trolley car?" Vivian asked.

"Good question, girl. It wasn't easy. We had to hice them up, in order to climb into cars or even to walk upstairs." I responded.

"I heard Mama say that when she was my age, people made pretty coloured drinking glasses and bottles. Why don't they make them today?" Vivian asked.

"Folks wanted to change to clear glass or a light green colour because no one could see through the dark bottles and glasses. They say that glass is real easy to make. Probably more for show than for service," I answered.

"They called it 'dark suncast' for pop bottles and things."

"Oh, I know. U'm Granny, what are prune shoes? What did they look and why did people call them prunes?" Genevieve asked.

Mom Suse almost dropped the large enamel bowl she was carrying the potatoes in. She plopped it on the table, real fast. Her sides were just about in stitches. Poor things, they didn't have a clue what they were talking about.

"My dear chile, I believe that the real call name was gaiters or spats; to protect the shoes. Yes, they were the colour of prunes," I explained, with a giggle. "You see, but we used to call them 'prunella shoes'. My, they sho' were comfortable. The boys wore what we used to call, 'hum-knit socks' on account of, they used to 'scour them out'. We girls wore thick, dark stockings, if we could afford them or else, home knit stockings," I explained.

"When you were a little girl, like us, what kind of dresses did you used to wear?" Inquired Vivian.

"In my mama's day, dresses were called mostly called frocks. We didn't have the capital to buy new stock so mama made all of our dresses. Mama got cross if we came from church and didn't change to our play clothes. She didn't want us going around looking like little vagrants.

The long, plain dresses were called delaine. Some were made with frills on the shoulders and hems. For church, we wore calico dresses which I thought were colourful and attractive," I explained.

"Wow, that sounds like a whole new set of words. Words I never heard before, and words I don't understand," confessed Vivian.

"That's alright honey, you don't have to understand," I said.

"It was a long time ago… in my day, anyway," I concluded.

Chapter 14

While Mom Suse and her family were singing 'Bringing in the Sheaves', her youngest daughter, Leota came strolling in through the back door.

'As I was approaching, I heard the sound of music coming from the house, so I knew we were going to have a fun time tonight," she said.

"Now that you're here Leota," said Papa.

"Why don't you play us a few songs on the organ, and we'll have a real old fashioned sing-song?"

"Sounds like a great idea," answered Leota.

"That's exactly what I had in mind, when I decided to come over here."

"Well, get to it, girl!" said Papa, anxious to relive some of the great family moments he cherished.

"Why don't you relax and have something to drink first. What would you like?" I asked.

"Just a cup of tea please," replied Leota.

"It's okay Granny Suse, I'll make auntie a cup of tea. Would anyone else like something to drink?" Barbara asked.

Leota put on the record, 'The Old Rugged Cross' on the gramophone. The Smith family sang along in perfect harmony. Barbara started singing with the rest of the family as she served the tea.

After Leota had finished her cup she sat down at the organ and began playing along with the record. The full sound created a musical buzz in the air. When the record was over, Leota asked, "Does anyone have a request? What about you, Pop?"

"I'd like to hear 'Down by the River Side'!" requested Papa. "I haven't heard it in along time, and I'd sure like to hear it now!"

The air was filled with their harmonious, voices. Yet, it was Papa Demus who had felt the most gratification. Due to his worsening blindness, he lost the freedom to play the organ. This depth of sound seemed to fill that longing in his soul. Besides, he had recently resigned his church position as chief organist. A position he held faithfully for over fifty years.

"That was a beautiful song, Demus," I said. "I'm glad you chose it."

"Why don't you choose another one, Suse?" he suggested, not wanting to have me left out of the fun.

"I'd like to hear, 'This Little Light of Mine', Leota," I said.

For Mom Suse and Papa Demus, the music reminded them of old times at the turn of the century. Nostalgia caused the old man to recall his earlier years as a young man playing the organ in local the church. In a few short minutes, Papa Demus was fast asleep.

The singsong in the parlour added realism to his dream where he accompanied the church choir in the rendition of 'Down by the Riverside'. The entire church resounded in angelic chorus.

"Look, Granny Suse," said Barbara, as the song was ending, "Papa Demus is sleeping!"

"He looks very peaceful, dear," I replied. "Don't disturb him – he probably needs his rest."

'Mom?" inquired Leota, "Maybe that's why we should stop playing the music."

"Ya' know, Leota," I said, as I looked at my adoring husband. "I think that at this time, your father would almost welcome a little music – I think he hears it, he looks content."

Leota began to play 'Amazing Grace'. The family joined in, but this time, it was more for the benefit of dear Papa Demus. However, during the midst of the song, Mom Suse noticed that her husband's breathing had become shallow.

"Stop the music! Stop singing!" I said with urgency. "I think there's something wrong with Demus – he isn't breathing. Please say it isn't so, God! It can't be!" I added in distress.

Mom Suse: Matriarch of the Preston area Black Communities

I quickly turned to see how he was doing. His breathing had become real faint.

"I think Demus has taken a turn for the worse. We better rush him to the hospital right away!" I exclaimed.

"Dennis, you go across the field and get your Uncle Joe to take your grandfather to the hospital. Tell him that his father has gotten worse, a lot worse – and hurry!"

"Uncle Joe! Uncle Joe!" screamed a frantic young Dennis.

"What's the matter, Dennis?" asked Joe.

"It's Grandad Demus!" said Dennis.

Dennis hurried back to tell Mom Suse that Joe would be right over.

"Oh! I'm glad you're here, Joe!" I said in relief. "Help me get your father into the truck quickly, so we can get him to the hospital! He's really sick this time!" I added.

All the way to the hospital Mom Suse was reassuring Papa Demus that everything was going to be all right. Her constant attention comforted his soul.

"Don't worry Demus," I said, "we'll soon have you to the hospital."

Upon arrival at the hospital, the attendants quickly put Papa Demus in a wheelchair, and whisked him away for examination in the emergency room. Afterwards, the attending doctor appeared.

"My name is Doctor John Savage, may I talk to you alone, Mrs. Smith?" He asked, politely.

"Of course, Dr. Savage," I replied.

Mom Suse followed the doctor down the hall and into his office.

"Can I be frank with you?" he asked.

"Of course," I answered.

"Your husband requires critical care. Pneumonia has set in Demus' lungs. He doesn't have much time left! It's just a matter of days..."

"Ah!" I gasped. "A matter of days... um, um, I was expecting this. He hasn't been well for about a week now," I added, in forlorn.

"We'll give him the best of care possible– don't you worry!" said the doctor.

"Thank you, but he's the *only* man I've ever loved. He's the *only* man I've every known. You don't know how much he means to me," I commented.

"Can… I, I see my husband, doctor?" I inquired, anxiously.

"Of course you can, Mrs. Smith," replied, the doctor. "Come with me and I'll walk you to him."

Demus was lying quietly in bed while the nurse watched over him. Mom Suse walked in and stood by his side.

"Is it alright if I take his hand in mine?" I asked.

"Certainly, Mrs. Smith, anything that'll make him feel more comfortable," replied the nurse. "He's resting now, but you may talk to him quietly, if you wish," she added.

Mom Suse took Papa Demus' hand in hers and spoke words of love and reassurance. The nurse offered her a chair.

"Demus, don't you worry, dear – everything's going to be just fine. We all love you and I'm by your side. I won't leave you, now dear!"

After a few hours of constant vigil, Mom Suse began to grow weary. The attending nurse kindly advised her to rest at home for a few hours.

"I really don't want to leave him, nurse," I said.

"I understand how you feel, Mrs. Smith, but your husband's condition seems a little better now. I think you can go home for a few hours rest. It'll do you a world of good, believe you me!" The nurse added.

"Only if you think that it's best. I'll go home and get some rest," I said, sadly.

Mom Suse got up to leave her husband's bedside then looked back in distress. When Joe drove his mother home, she cried, uncontrollably throughout the entire journey. This was truly the saddest time of her life, a time to seek consolation from the heart of God.

Incidentally, Mom Suse's daily relationship with God, proved to be her saving grace.

"We're back home, Mom. Let me walk you inside and stay awhile," said a concerned Joe.

"Thank you Joe, that would be fine," I commented.

When she entered the house, her daughter Leota was there to greet her.

"Come in, Mom," said Leota. "How's Pop? Is he going to be okay?"

"He's very, very weak, Leota," was all that I could say.

"Let me make you a cup of tea, Mom," said Leota.

"That'll be fine, dear," I responded. "I feel so-o sad."

"Mom, I think that after a good night's sleep, you'll feel much better," encouraged my youngest daughter.

"Thanks, Leota," I said. "I'm glad you and the grandchildren are here with me – I couldn't go through this alone."

"I'll stay overnight with you, if you'd like, Mom," said Leota.

"That's some kind of girl," I said. I think I'll go up to bed now."

Not until Leota was certain her mother was asleep, did she retire to the spare room adjacent to her parent's room. But Mom Suse had not yet fallen asleep. Her immediate concern was to seek out the Great Physician, and ask for His will concerning her husband. The Good Lord had never failed her in the past, and she was certain that he wasn't about to start now.

The traumatic day's events caused her to fall into a deep sleep. Mom Suse had an unusual mystical experience. For her, it was a source of both comfort and enlightenment. In her dream she was a young lady again, playing with her eldest daughter Etta, who had died of tuberculosis, during the Depression.

"You're all right, Etta – you're not dead!" I said, in surprise.

"Of course I'm alright, Mom," said Etta, rather emphatically.

"She's very good," said a man's voice that came from behind me.

Mom Suse had a startled expression as she looked around to see who was who was speaking to her. A very kind man with long hair tied in a ponytail, stood there before her. He had the kindest face that she had ever seen. She was immediately at ease with him.

"I hope that I didn't frighten you, my dear," said the man. "Everyone here has been chosen by me, as have you and your husband, Demus," he said, in an authoritative voice.

Mom Suse didn't know whether it was the man's bearing or his tone of voice, but she had peace of mind. She didn't question his word - it gave her comfort.

"How do you know my husband?" I asked, humbly.

"I've known your family all of their lives," was the reply.

It was then, that Mom Suse realized she was in the presence of the Living God. She bowed down before Him and cried, uncontrollably. She told Him of her grief regarding her husband's failing health.

"You're a good woman, Susannah," was His reply. "If you stand before me, I will answer your questions."

She felt a sudden suspension of her grief; it was temporarily replaced by her unquenchable thirst for knowledge.

"What's going to become of Demus? Lord, what's going to become of my husband?" I implored.

"Susannah, Demus will soon be in this beautiful garden with your daughters, Etta and Adeline," he replied.

"It's truly beautiful here, Lord," was all I could say.

All at once, Etta and Adeline appeared before her. They were gorgeous women, more beautiful than words could express. Mom Suse was so overcome with joy at seeing her two daughters standing before her.

They were totally illuminated by a golden light. Instinctly, she ran over to embrace them, and call out their names.

"Etta! Adeline! I thought that I'd never see the two of you again!" I said, thoroughly delighted.

"You girls are so-o beautiful!"

"So are you, Mom," they answered, in unison.

Mom Suse looked down into a shimmering pool of water that appeared before her. In it she saw, a crystal clear reflection of herself as a lovely young lady. She had looked more attractive than she had every remembered. As God spoke with Mom Suse, there was sheer delight on her face her.

"Susannah, everyone here is lovely. What you have seen here is actually what you really are inside – a pure heart. Soon Demus will be with us in this attractive garden. He'll be enjoying himself like all the others – until one day when you return here reunited with him in eternal love".

The inhabitants all seemed to have a place in that beautiful garden. In that moment, the anxiety of Demus's health, and the concern for her family had dissipated.

Mom Suse: Matriarch of the Preston area Black Communities

Mom Suse's experience had transformed her fears into a haven of peace. She had awakened from her heavenly dream - alone again, in the darkness of her bedroom. Yet, the blessedness bestowed upon her remained within.

"I feel alright," I said, to myself. "I know what the future holds for Demus and myself. I also understand that there is something special awaiting each one of us."

Before entering her mom's bedroom, Leota gently knocked at the door. She heard a bit of movement coming from within.

"Is everything okay, Mom?" asked Leota.

"Everything is fine, dear," I answered.

"I've just been blessed and I know that everything's going to be okay for our family. We all have a purpose – a good purpose. So I have to be at my best when I see Demus next," I added.

The following day came early for Mom Suse. She ate her breakfast quickly while Leota helped her feed the children. After which, Joe drove his mother back to the hospital. Mom Suse recounted to Joe the events of her previous night's dream. Joe listened carefully, but if the truth be told, he was spellbound. He didn't respond until Mom Suse told him the entire dream.

"That's an incredible story Mom," said Joe. "It's very touching! If what you say is true, then this family is blest," he added.

"It's all true, Joe," I stated, "Just as He told me. What I've experienced in that dream has caused me to feel so wonderful," I added.

"We're here Mom, let's hope Pop's felling better," said Joe, optimistically.

As Dr. Savage walked by, Mom Suse and Joe entered the hospital.

"Good morning, Mrs. Smith," said the physician. "I hope you had a good rest."

"I did doctor, thank you," I answered.

"Doctor Savage, tell me something, do you think miracles can happen?"

"I believe so, Mrs. Smith. Under these circumstances, I d..."

Mom Suse quickly answered, seeing that Doctor Savage didn't quite understand what she meant.

"Can I tell you an unusual dream that I had last night?" I asked.

"Go right ahead, Mrs. Smith!" was his reply.

Mom Suse shared her dream with him. He did not respond until a couple of minutes had past. "You're a fortunate woman, Mrs. Smith – very fortunate indeed. Yes, I do sort of believe in those kinds of miracles, but that's strictly off the record. Modern science cannot explain them, but I do believe in God, and I do think He does 'move in mysterious ways,' as the Bible says. If you find inspiration from this dream, then good for you, and I think that you should abide by its teachings," said the doctor.

"Thanks doctor," I said. I really do feel inspired by the dream, but I think it was more than a regular dream. I believe that God, in His mercy is comforting me, so I can be there for Demus. He needs me so much now," I said.

"Why don't you go in and see your husband, now, Mrs. Smith?" said the doctor. "He might be awake, so perhaps, you can get to talk to him."

Papa Demus was resting when Mom Suse entered his room. His eyes were open and they lit up when he heard his wife's voice.

"Good morning Demus," I said, and walked over to his beside. I kissed his cheek, and held his hand.

"You're looking just fine, just fine!" I commented said, trying to cheer him up.

"I feel fine, Suse," answered Demus, rather faintly.

"Is there anything I can get you dear?" I inquired.

"Yes, I would like a sip of water or juice," answered Demus

"I'd be happy to, dear," I answered. Then I got up to press the buzzer near his bed.

In a few moments, a nurse arrived.

"Is there anything I can get you?" she asked and busied herself with Demus's care.

"Will you please bring Demus some juice, nurse?" I asked.

"Sure thing," replied the nurse. Would you like something too, Mrs. Smith?"

"I wouldn't mind a cup of tea," I replied.

Mom Suse: Matriarch of the Preston area Black Communities

"No trouble at all, Mrs. Smith," replied the nurse, as she left the room.

"Now that we're alone, Demus, I'd like to tell you how much I love you," I said, and placed my hand on his.

"I love you, too," said Demus. "You were always so good to me and the children," he added.

"I'm glad you think so, Demus, cause you've always been the best husband that I could wish for, and our children have had the best father, ever," I said.

A moment later the nurse returned with the beverages.

"Here you are Mrs. Smith," as she handed me the cup of tea. Then she gave Demus his juice, which he gratefully accepted.

When the nurse left the room, Mom Suse began to share her dream with Papa Demus. He had always been closer to her than anyone else, and he understood the importance of its significance.

"You're blessed, my dear," replied Demus.

"So are you," I recalled. "The blessing was extended to our entire family."

For the last few weeks of Papa Demus' life, he was in critical care. Mom Suse, and her children kept a constant rotating vigil at his hospital bedside. It all ended, too abruptly, the day the illness snuffed out his last breath.

"Demus," I said. "I'm right by your side. I hope that you can hear me. I won't leave you alone, so don't worry about a thing."

Papa Demus looked up, too weak to acknowledge his wife's presence. He desperately wanted to speak, but the words couldn't make it past his lips. Their daughter, Pauline, soon joined the couple.

"How's Pop?" Pauline asked.

"He's still terribly weak," I answered. "He tried to speak, but the words wouldn't come out."

Pauline went over to the other side of her papa's bed. She gazed fondly at her, dear old dad, with lasting memories.

"Pop! It's Pauline, Pauline!" she said, gently.

Papa Demus followed Pauline's voice and smiled in recognition. Once again, he attempted to speak, but without success.

"Don't try to speak, Pop," said Pauline. "I'm here and I love you very much. Is there anything I can get you?"

"Why don't you see if you can find him some unsweetened orange juice?" I asked.

Mom Suse sat for several minutes staring lovingly at her husband of over fifty glorious years. Many memories were conjured up in those few brief moments, only to be jarred by the sweet return of Pauline.

"This is unsweetened orange juice, Mom," said Pauline. "Pop's lips look very parched. I think this will be just the thing he needs."

Pauline patiently fed her dad the juice, making sure that he didn't drink too much, at once.

"He looks a little better now since he's had his juice," I noted.

"I wanted to get him some, but I didn't want to leave him, not even for a moment. If I had left the room, I was afraid something might happen to him," I said.

"You've been under a lot of strain lately, Mom, I think you'd better go home for a little while and get some rest, don't you?" Pauline asked.

So it was with great reluctance that Mom Suse left Papa Demus' side and returned home.

"Do you want me to go with you, Mom?" asked Pauline.

"No! I think I'll be alright by myself," I replied. "I'd like you to stay with your father just in case he might need something. I don't really like leaving him alone, in case something happens," I concluded.

"Okay, Mom! I think you're right! I wouldn't want anything to happen to Pops, especially with no one around," added Pauline.

"When I go home, I'll see to it that the grandchildren have something to eat," I said.

"Leota fed and sent them off to school, before I got here," recalled Pauline. "But you know kids are – they are always hungry!"

"I sure know that after all these years," I noted, with a little cheer in my voice.

She loved her grandchildren. Their needs were always foremost in her mind, even now, at a time like this.

No sooner had Mom Suse left the hospital grounds then her son, Joe pulled up in his truck.

"I was just coming to see how Pop was doing," said Joe.

"Well I'm going home to get some rest and see about the grandchildren," said a tired Mom Suse.

"Okay, come on Mom, let's get you back home," said Joe. After Joe dropped his Mom home, he intended to return to the hospital, and relieve his sister Pauline for, at least, a few hours.

"If you're going to be there that long," I said, "why don't you come in and let me make you a sandwich or two to take with you?"

"Sounds like a good idea, Mom," said Joe. "I am feeling kinda hungry after just coming from work."

A few hours rest was all that Mom Suse required. She woke up completely refreshed. Her mind was thoroughly consumed with thinking about returning to the hospital. She needed to be by Demus's bedside. Quickly, she fixed herself something to eat along with the few sandwiches. As she was putting the finishing touches on her sandwiches when Leota came to see if her mother needed anything.

"Leota I was just about to return to the hospital to stay by your father's side. I don't like to leave him for too long," I said.

""I just came from there, Mom. He was resting nicely and Joe is sitting with him now," reported Leota.

"Joe's been there a long time," I said. "I think I'd better hurry on over and relieve him. I'm anxious to see how he is – I worry about him so. O Lord, you know that he's all I have in this world!" I whispered.

Without warning, she broke down and started to cry. Leota held her close and let her cry out all the sorrow that had been bottled up since Papa Demus' hospital stay.

"I don't want to lose him, Leota," I cried.

"It'll be alright, Mom," said Leota. "Pop's getting the best of care. Please don't worry," she encouraged.

"Leota, I really think that I'd better get going," I said. "But first I'd better freshen up. I can't let Demus see me like this. I'd better get a grip on myself."

Leota took her mother to the hospital. When Mom Suse arrived, Joe was sitting by his fathers' side. Demus was sleeping. When Joe saw his mother, he arose to greet her.

"He's sleeping now, Mom," whispered Joe. He was asking for you, a little after you left. But he's been sleeping for some time now."

"I'm glad you were here with him, Joe," I said. "It wouldn't have been of good, if he awakened with no one around."

"That's what I thought too, Mom," said Joe. "I was really happy to hear his voice. When he heard me, he smiled. It made me feel real good to be here."

Joe stayed for a little while longer. He looked at Mom Suse. Her face revealed the burden on her soul.

Papa Demus opened his eyes, and instinctly knew that Mom Suse was beside him.

"Hello, Suse!" said Demus, in his faint voice.

"Hello, Demus!" I said, as I took his hand in mine.

"How are you feeling, dear?" I asked.

"Tired!" replied the very weak Demus.

"Don't try to speak too much, honey," I assured. "It's so nice to see that you're awake. I didn't want to leave you alone for long, but I was so tired that I had to go home to catch up on a little sleep.

"That's alright, Suse. I was sleeping too," noted Demus, with a faint smile.

"I'd like some tea, Suse," requested Demus. "'Cause my throat feels dry."

"I'll step into the hall for a moment, to see if there's a nurse around," I said. "I'll be right back honey."

" A nurse walked by as Mom Suse stepped into the hall.

"Nurse!" I exclaimed. "Could you bring my husband some tea? Oh and, no sugar, please."

"Honey, I just saw the nurse," I said. "She'll be back shortly with your tea."

"That's fine, Suse," said Demus, with a little smile.

Mom Suse sat with Papa Demus and continued to hold his hand.

"Is there anything else I can get for you, Mrs. Smith?" asked the nurse.

"No dear," I. "We're just fine, now. Thank you!"

Mom Suse patiently, fed Papa Demus his tea. He sipped it with great difficulty. Her undying love for him provided him with the comfort he needed. After Papa Demus finished his tea, he looked over at his wife, smiled and closed his eyes. Mom Suse continued to drink her tea, while looking lovingly at her Papa Demus, who slept soundly.

"Oh no, Lord God! Don't tell me that his breathing has stopped!" I whispered.

This sudden change of events startled her to the point where she accidentally dropped her cup of tea. She called for a nurse to check up on Papa Demus' condition.

"Nurse! Nurse! Come quick! Demus has stopped breathing! Please hurry!" I said, very frantically.

Instantly, a nurse rushed into the room, while another went to search for the night doctor on call. Mom Suse quickly went back into Papa Demus' room so see what the nurse could do.

"I don't feel any pulse," said the nurse, in surprise. "The doctor's on his way!" she said. "He'll know what to do!"

A few anxious moments later, the doctor entered the room.

"The patient has no pulse." Exclaimed the nurse.

"Let me have a look," said the doctor. He quickly checked Papa Demus for vital signs. After a lengthy examination, the doctor looked up at Mom Suse and shook his head in despair.

"I'm sorry, Mrs. Smith. He's gone!" noted the doctor, sympathetically.

"There was nothing else that could have been done. Once pneumonia sets in, it's just a matter of time before the lungs give out. If it's any comfort, he did seem to pass away peacefully," added, Dr. Savage.

The doctor then left Mom Suse alone with Papa Demus. As soon as the door was closed, she began to cry releasing some of her pent up anguish. She began calling out Papa Demus' name in between heavy bouts of grief.

A while later, there was a knock on Papa Demus' room door. The doctor advised her that her family had been notified of their father's death. Mom Suse was alone again with the body of her dear, departed husband.

Suddenly, there appeared a faint glow over Papa Demus' body. It was very hypnotic and commanded Mom Suse's full attention. The opaque glow seemed to take on a human form. As it did, she felt an abiding love at seeing Papa Demus' smiling face.

This was God's method of comfort to her. At once, the weighty burden of grief released itself from her being. It was replaced by a sense of serenity. The vision she had just experienced renewed her faith in God. A God, whose presence was evident during their entire forty-four years of their marriage.

Her youngest son, Joe drove his newly widowed mother home.

"You seem calm Mom, almost relaxed," said the bewildered Joe.

"I've seen your father, Joe," I said, "and he's very happy now that he's in heaven!"

"Ya' know, Mom I feel a lot better, now that I've heard you tell me about you new vision," replied Joe.

Mom Suse arrived back home to a house full of family members. Their presence comforted her and renewed her strength. She shared her most recent vision with them as the folks gave her their undivided attention.

Night had fallen and folks slowly dispersed to their respective homes leaving Mom Suse and Pauline alone. Sensing her mother's profound loss, Pauline decided to stay the night. While Mom Suse slept, she experienced yet, another vision. In this instance, Papa Demus appeared to her as a dashing young man wearing a fashionable suit. Mom Suse was seized with an unexplainable excitement at feeling like a young bride again. The handsome Demus Smith flashed her one of his winsome smiles. Of course, he was more attracted to her iridescent, internal beauty.

This elated sensation served to inspired Mom Suse, for years to come. It mingled itself with her unyielding love for the Lord. She dealt with her sorrow of loosing Papa Demus on a daily basis, and God Almighty never disappointed her.

Chapter 15

Demus Smith past away in 1948. His body had been taken to the local funeral parlour for preparation. The Wake was held at the family residence. On the third day, the hearse arrived at the family residence to take the body of dear, departed Demus Smith, to St. Thomas United Baptist for the funeral service given by Rev. A.A. Wyse.

By the time the Reverend stepped up to the pulpit, the church had already filled to capacity. The sermon was an eloquent tribute to the Late Demus Smith was born in 1878, married in 1904 and past away in 1948. Papa Demus lived for seventy good, long years. At the time of Papa Demus' death, Mom Suse had not long reached her sixty-fifth birthday. Following the service, the committal took place at the St. Thomas Baptist Church Cemetery.

In the weeks following the funeral, life went on as usual at the farm. Little time was left for reflection. In the course of serving her regular customers, Mom Suse continued to receive many words of condolences. Her family was of great comfort. Needless to say, her children often worried about their mother's health. They promised to never leave her alone whether around the homestead, or accompanying her on rounds with customers.

Whenever Mom Suse found it too hard to carry on without her Demus, she would recall the days of her ancestors. Mom Suse realized that, Divine Intervention lit the paths of fugitive slaves who sacrificed their lives. She clearly understood that if the ancestors they had not paved the way, then her good fortune in life probably, would not have existed. Had it not been for the thousand of escapees who 'travelled' the 'Underground Railroad', the countless others who reached Nova Scotia as ship stowaways and other routes, our daily paths would *not* have been illuminated.

The years directly following the Second World War brought much commercial gain to Canada. Thanks to the upsurge in the economy, the Smith Farm hired more than thirty employees. Finally, all the years of hard work paid off. For the first time, Mom Suse was able to relax and enjoy the fruits of her labour. She was not one to put her feet up and watch the world go by. Instead, Mom Suse utilized her time at the Ladies Auxillary, the Church Choir, True Blue Club, Helping Hand Society, etc. The last noted, non-profit society, provided second-hand clothing and non-perishable provisions to the needy.

Mom Suse had often helped to distribute these items. There were times where she would re-assure the recipients that, although they found themselves in need, God had still blessed them with life!

The church had always been Mom Suse's mainstay. At times, she assisted Rev. Wyse with baptisms. Fortunately, the old tradition of sending the baptismal candidates into the woods for the purpose of interpreting their dreams as being inspired had gone by the wayside.

Mom Suse enjoyed preparing meals and entertaining local guests or those 'from-away'. Her heart was into everything she did. From Friday afternoon until Sunday morning, the kitchen was the busiest room in the house. She began cooking enough food to feed the whole congregation. After the guests partaken had eaten it was customary, to converse late into the night.

Mom Suse and her eldest daughter Helen, shared a conversation.

"Wow, I see that there's a telephone number for Cornwallis Street Baptist Church. It's under Rev. Oliver's name," reported Helen.

"That's all fine and dandy, but it doesn't do us any good. We don't have a phone. I hear that the contraption is nothing but a 'gossip line'," I commented.

"Folks in town tell me that the phone line works on a party system. For a one-party line, a family is serviced with fifteen calls daily. The two-party line gives the home twelve calls daily, and the three-party line, only offers them eight calls per day. In case of an emergency, just dial 'O', to reach the operator." I recalled.

"But Mama, what do you mean by 'the gossip lines'?" asked Helen.

"Oh that," I said. "For each party line there is a certain ring. If I pick the phone on a different ring, by mistake or because I **want** to be noisy, I can hear everybody else's conversation. That's what I call 'the gossip line'. I mean, I'm not going to pay for a phone system that I'm sharing with people."

Once again, another fire consumed the Smith's family home. This time, a grandchild playing with matches the flame ignited the flames. The damage confined itself to the upper level. The appetite of this fire was not as voracious as the fire of the '40's, which consumed the entire house. Oh no, this fire seemed to show a bit more respect. It was with the help of family and friends, that this last home was rebuilt as a large bungalow. By God' grace, there were no casualties in these two disasters. This was the fire of the early 1950's.

Mom Suse was enjoying a quiet moment of extending greetings as she sat on her porch. She seemed to have recognized the form of the minister.

"Mercy me," she said softly, "that man's gonna walk his way right into the pearly gates!"

"How you doing Rev. Wyse? Now, you just sit yourself down here, while I go in and fetch you a tall glass of lemonade. Do you want a couple slices of lemon or banana loaf to go with it? I'll bring some anyway," I said.

A few minutes later, Mom Suse returned to the porch and placed a couple trays of goodies on the table. It consisted of two tall glasses of lemonade, a saucer piled with lemon, cherry loaf and banana bread. Another saucer was decorated with pump and juicy red grapes surrounded with bite-size chunks of cheddar cheese.

The minister stepped inside to wash his hands, sat back on the porch and thanked his gracious hostess. Rev. Wyse promptly said the grace, and had a bite to eat. As long as his flock took care of him – and they did. He didn't mind the walking which kept him fit. Sometimes he was fortunate enough to hitch a ride on a horse and buggy. Or the odd time, he was a passenger in one of the few vehicles, in the community.

"Rev. Wyse, how are things with you these days? I hope and pray that your faith will remain strong, regardless," I exhorted.

"Mom Suse, I'm suppose to be the one pasturing you," said the minister, with a little smile.

"We'll Reverend, we are all in the same boat, so we might as well help on another. All I've got to say is, God is Good! " I added.

"All the time," chorused the reverend.

"Mom Suse, I hear that you have a new grandson… and he's some good looking. Congratulations! He exclaimed.

"Thank you, Reverend, another blessing from our Maker, but my grandson's looks will be the least of his problems," I added.

"I know what you mean," he responded, in agreement.

"Well, well, Reverend what do you make of this new contraption they call, the television set? They say it's like having a little picture screen in your home," I commented.

"That's right, but the only thing is that the programs are filmed 'live'. Right there and then, at the television studio," said the Reverend. "I can't say that I'm interested. It's too costly, anyway. I don't think that I'll miss what I've never had," he added.

"And I agree," I said.

"Do you know, that Israel is looking to be recompensed from Germany for her losses during the Second World War," I said.

"Um, I can't say that I blame them any. It makes me think about us black folks. Will we ever by recompensed for our losses regarding slavery, not to mention our present struggles? And the Natives – what about them? The many injustices that still, I say, still continue and, all in the name of Jesus. Will we ever be recompensed or is it only for folks who are clothed in white skin?" enquired the Reverend.

"That's a pain *too hard* for them to bear… or admit. It hard to admit that your forefathers continued in racism of some form or another. Or perhaps were either slave masters or somehow engaged in the slave trade," I said.

"Too hard for them to bear? Too hard for *them* to bear," repeated the minister, in anguish. For hundreds and hundreds of years, we had to pass through the depths of hottest hell. And, they don't think that was too hard for *us*?" He paused a moment. "At some point, God expects man to come to grips with past events. If unacknowledged then the issues will *never* be resolved. We must *all* face our demons, especially of *past generational sins*.

"Um hm, only God can save," I said.

"And only God *did* save," added Rev. Wyse.

"Our strength is eternal," I noted.

"Yes, and our strength came and *still* comes from God, himself!" concluded the Reverend.

On several occasions, Mom Suse related stories about her childhood to her children and grandchildren. One of these talks took place when her granddaughter, Vivian Willis, came over to visit. At first, the things that were said were quite ordinary.

"Granny, in your day, women didn't have their babies in hospitals, did they?" asked Vivian.

"Oh no, in this community that was unheard of until the mid-fifties with the construction of the Angus L. Macdonald Bridge. In my day, our midwives

were Cousin Sophie Diggs Wilson and Kitty Willis. By the way, Kitty was your great grandmother. We also had Lucie Beals and Barbara Provo," I noted.

Then Mom Suse said something that sounded unbelievably strange. So strange, that Vivian raised her eyebrows and gasped. The question caught her by surprise.

"Did you know that when I was a child, there was still slavery going on in Nova Scotia?" I asked, candidly.

"I thought slavery ended at the close of the Civil War," said a bewildered Vivian.

"That's what Mama Pauline taught me. And as for slavery in Canada, I thought that it ended a lot earlier than the late eighteenth century. Mama said that, here in Nova Scotia, slavery was ended in early 1800's"

"I'm sorry to disillusion you, dear," I said. "Slavery should have ended somewhere around 1829 to 1834. But, it didn't. It ended, instead in the late 1890's when I was a child. Vivian, there's a lot of things people don't know about, that us old-timers remember. Our people were publicly auctioned as slaves, right here in Halifax at the

Farmer's Market. Young lady, if you think nowadays is bad, back then, they used to treat our people some foul. Um, um, um and some things are better left unsaid. Our girls, especially, were unmercifully used as sex slaves. When their masters got them pregnant, those girls were cast out like useless pieces of garbage," I concluded.

"Say what!" Exclaimed Vivian.

"Imagine, I was a child, and I *saw* the slave masters, pawing those folks at the auction block. All manner of evil, I tell you. And to think, they used to look on us with murderous eyes… when **they** were doing us wrong!" I recalled.

"Granny, I knew that our people were persecuted for a long, long time, but what you've told me is absolutely horrifying," said Vivian.

"The saddest of all is to see our own men as slave masters. There were a few, but the curse of it all! I guess they didn't want to be slaves so they decided to become masters. What a disgrace to the race!" I said, in anguish.

"There were laws against such practices, but where blacks were concerned, I guess, some white people just didn't care! Thank goodness, it's a lot better now than what it was. But it's still going to have to get even better, before things are the way that God meant them to be," I said.

"I sure hope change takes place in my lifetime!" said Vivian.

"So do I dear," I exclaimed. "So do I!"

"Sweetie, I remember that months before the Great War, or the First World War that Halifax believed that it had a crises on is hand," I reported.

"What kind of crises, the sinking of the 'Titantic' or the Halifax Explosion?"

"Neither one. The 'Titantic' sank in April of 1912, and the Halifax Explosion occurred December of 1917. No, this event was called the 'Asian Invasion'," I recalled.

"Granny, what on earth is the 'Asian Invasion'? It sounds like the name of a television show. I never heard tell of that before," added Vivian

"Chile, there are something's that the white man would rather forget ever happened," I said, emphatically.

"Yea, like slavery in Nova Scotia," quipped a frustrated Vivian.

Mom Suse: Matriarch of the Preston area Black Communities

I smiled. "Vivian," I thought, "was a 'chip off the old block."

"Your Grandpa Demus, God rest the dead," I recalled, "told us about a boat load of 500 Hindus. They were making their way to Halifax. Well, if the Canadian authorities weren't in an uproar. They called it the 'Asian Invasion'. Demus said that the upcoming war would cause us to loose much more than 500 Canadians. He believed that they should have brought them on in. Don't you know that the Canadian government put forth an undertaking, to keep the Hindu's out of Canada, and sent back to India!" recounted.

"What? Really, Granny Suse, you mean to tell me that the government was just that mean?" Exclaimed Vivian.

"Vivian, do you recall the times that I spoke to you about my Grandpappy Cain?"

"I recall some, Granny. Maybe I was too young, said Vivian.

"No matter." I said. "You're not bound to hold onto everything I tell you. When I was a young girl, in the late 1890's, I'd spent some time at my grandparent's house, Mama Annie and Papa Daniel. I often slept in the bedroom that was situated above the parlour. If you bent down low, you could peak and see where folks sat and hear big people's discussions, which was *none* of my business. Okay Vivian, I'm guilty of being an eavesdropper! Anyway, young lady, I've always told you fellas that nobody's perfect. Especially, not your dear, old granny. Well, on his particular evening, Mama Annie was sitting on the sofa, real comfortable. I could see that she was knitting, 'cause when she finished she used, what we called, 'bone caps' to protect the ends of her knitting needles.

"I couldn't see Papa Daniel. He sat on the opposite side," I noted.

"Granny Suse, what did you hear?" asked Vivian, somewhat impatiently.

"Now hush, young lady, and learn to be patient," I rebuked, lovingly.

"Alright, Granny Suse, you take your time," said Vivian, respectfully.

"Mama Annie asked Papa Daniel that when he was a slave on the Alabama plantation, did he ever yell out while being whipped?" I recalled.

"What was Papa Daniel's answer?" asked Vivian, in anticipation.

"Yes and no!" He responded.

"What? How can that be? Quizzed Vivian, with arched eyebrows.

"Now, well this was your great grandpappy's answer," I said.

"No, because if anyone yelled, cried or showed any fear, they'd be whupped 'til they either they shut up or 'til the torture shut them up... forever. Yes, I recited. Papa Daniel said that he yelled, cried as loud he could... deep, deep *within* his soul."

"So Mama Annie asked him, again, "Sweetie, so then, you mean that the added torture shut you up?" I revealed.

I related Papa Daniel's answer. "No baby, don't you know that a heart can cry, yell and shout, without making a single sound. Even, without a shedding a single tear?"

"So that's how it's all possible," said Vivian.

"Do you know what was worse of it?" I asked.

"No Granny Suse," replied Vivian.

"Papa Daniel would always ask, "If Canada is the 'Land of Freedom', then how come there's slavery up here, in Nova Scotia?" I quoted.

Dear old Rev. W. Wyse had long since past away, but not forgotten. At times, Reverend Wyse had ministered to the Campbell Road Church in Africville. Time after time, he would faithfully walk from the Preston area back to Bedford Basin.

The new minister, Reverend Donald Skeir, succeeded him as pastor of the three Preston area churches: East Preston, North Preston and Cherry Brook. Rev. Skeir, had a dual profession, he also worked as a schoolteacher. The minister parked his car in the Smith's driveway, sauntered toward the house and knocked on the door. Mom Suse recently arrived home from one of her church meetings. In fact, she was just taking off her overcoat when she heard the knock. With her dear, departed Demus gone, she was always glad for some company at end of the day. The parlour was just the place to be. After the normal niceties, the conversation was free to travel in any direction.

"It sure is good to hear that Dr. Martin Luther King, received the Noble Peace Price," said a proud Reverend.

"Hm, he worked hard enough for it, harder than anyone else that I know," I recalled.

"Isn't it amazing to know that when the Canadian government decided to end racial segregation in schools. Our little province of Nova Scotia was the last to integrate? Now, what does that say?" Asked Rev. Skeir.

"It says a whole lot, and we can read between the lines," I responded.

"I can't begin to imagine the fear that our Africville children faced during their integratiing days," commented Reverend Skeir.

"All the way to Richmond Street? That's a mighty big hill for short little legs to climb," I said.

The minister was now speaking in his capacity as a teacher.

"I'm reminded of our one-room school house back in the day. It was quite a struggle for our children. The highest grade level offered was either Grade 7 or 8, and the students tried hard to get by," replied the teacher.

"Good thing they didn't have to deal with integration; that would have been the undoing of many," I added.

"Mom Suse, it's a funny thing about the overall education in this province. It seems like the religious tension that peaked in the 'Old World' never quite dissipated here, in the 'New World'. It's like this, the early Nova Scotian pioneers continued to promote religious segregation in education. You see, even nowadays, students attend either a Catholic or a Protestant institution (at all levels). It seems as though society isn't working hard enough to create a harmonious atmosphere," commented the minister.

"I'm hopeful that in time, things will change," I stated. "I'm hopeful that things will change."

"Hm, Lord have mercy and in the house of God on a Sunday morning," said the Reverend. And he seemed his heart was clearly breaking. "Folks down in Alabama say it was the Ku Klux Klan. Deep in your bones, you know that it was them," added Rev. Skeir.

"Um hm, my grandfather used to be slave on one of those old plantations, in Alabama. That place was something else! Now you hear that the KKK bombed the church and took the lives of four little black girls? Um, um, um, Lord have mercy on the family. Mind ya', Mrs. Ash was telling me about that foul group of thugs, they're absolutely, good for nothing," I said.

"I know that you've heard about the fate of that unfortunate coal miner in Glace Bay. The black man who was burned alive, in a ball field?" I asked.

"What! Here in Nova Scotia?" Rev. Skeir questioned, in shock.

"Yes, That's right. A black coal miner was on his way home from work with a group of his mining buddies. It's probable that they all spent sometime in a nearby bar. Well, something evil took place and the poor fella was 'marked'. His 'buddies' set him right on fire. They left him there in the ball field, 'til he turned to ashes. Right on the ball field! That's where he died. That's *how* he died." I reported. "Lord have mercy, on his soul!"

"Burned alive?" Asked Rev. Skeir, obviously in shock.

"Um hm. The next day, his fellow miners claimed to know nothing of the incident. They *all* claimed to know *nothing*." I concluded.

"You know, it's about time that society acknowledge their part in our past; it's also *their* past. To be in constant denial is live a constant lie. Healing can be present when both sides acknowledge past wrongs. It's the groundwork towards forgiveness. We need to move forward, together," he concluded.

"And look here! The government has taken the land right out from Africville. There's so much commotion is this old world – Jesus has to come soon!" I exclaimed, in a weary tone.

"The last man standing was ole Pa Carvery. Thank God that he received a reasonable settlement... with the help of our black organizations," said Rev. Skeir.

"He wasn't going anywhere empty-handed. They couldn't fool *him*, no siree. Last man standing," I reiterated.

The Post-War Re-development Plans in North America aimed at decongesting not only the traffic arteries in a downtown core, but to distribute the ever-growing populace. The design of subdivisions, and large shopping centres, would serve to produce suburban communities.

Hence, urban planning committees scheduled and re-development, at least, twenty years in advance, and Halifax was no exception.

"Mama, remember Cassius Clay? He became a Muslim, changed his religion and his name?" asked Joe.

"Um, can't forget something like that. He did all that changing and still, went round acting all biggyfied. Those changes didn't seem to make him more humble," she said. "Grant it, he *is* one of the greatest boxers of all time," I added.

"He's a man of his word. He stands up for his beliefs!" said Joe. "Looky here, when he refused to bear arms in the Vietnam War, they stripped him of his boxing title, and threw him in jail. But he returned to the ring to regain it. Now, what does that say?" asked Joe, beaming with pride.

Joe had ways just like his father. He asked a question and didn't wait for your answer.

"Remember when he fought George Chuvalo? Did you know that he's a Native Canadian?" Joe inquired.

"Sure, they had two fights. The first in '66 and the last in '72, that took place in Vancouver. Don't you know that the Indian's face ended up looking like mush?"

"Oh Joe, you don't have to be so, so you know?" I pleaded while squinting my eyes in pain.

"Okay, Ma' I'm sorry, but what I'm saying is that Ali didn't have a single mark on his face," explained Joe.

"So," I said, "what was Clay's problem?"

"He thought that he'd teach Chuvalo a lesson. When they were in the ring, Chuvalo kept calling him Cassius Clay, just like you do, Mama," joked Joe.

"Are you trying to be a smart alec?" I teased.

"Do you recall how much money they made from that last match?" I asked.

"Yes ma'am," answered Joe. "Chuvalo made near $70,000.00 and Ali took home about $200,000.00. Not bad, eh?"

"We have our own boxers, right here in Nova Scotia, like Buddy Daye, from New Glasgow. He won the Canadian Jr. Lightweight in '64, I believe.

Don't forget about Clyde Gray, from 'down-the-line', in Three Mile Plains. He won the Commonwealth Welterweight Championship title in '79," Joe bragged.

As Mom Suse became aged, but remained mentally astute she continued to live in the community on a rotating basis with three of her daughters (Helen, Pauline and Ruth).

"Mama," said Pauline, "I was talking to Vivian in Toronto, and she says they've got a doctor up there who performs abortions. One time, the police jailed him, for under two years, I think. Anyway, when he got out, didn't turn around and do the same thing?"

"Um, um, um, in my day, a woman would be more discreet about wanting to get rid of her child. Nowadays, it all seems a little too common. Back in my day, some women tried to operate on themselves. Of course, after that attempt, many didn't live to see light of day," I said, regretfully.

"Hm, Mama I'm sure glad we got rid of those old party line phones. These new private lines are just perfect," said a satisfied Pauline. "Mama, did you regret not owning a telephone or a television set?" asked Pauline.

"Honey, I've never known life with them. I don't miss what I never had," I replied.

"Well, I'm sure you're missing the pure gospel music of Mahalia Jackson, she probably touched a lot of souls," commented Pauline.

"Not to mention Louis Armstrong, oh well, he was great! Had a real genuine smile," added Pauline.

"That fine, young singer who died in a plane crash, in the early 70's, Pauline what was his name?" I inquired.

"Oh you must mean, Otis Redding.

"What was the name of his song?" I asked.

"'When a Man Loves a Woman," replied Pauline. "Man, that cat could really sing!"

"Oh girl, that song always puts me in mind of your dear, departed father. "Um, um, um," I gladly, reminisced. "Um um um, he sure knew how to love this woman"

Chapter 16

"Mama, do you recall telling me about the Shubenacadie Indian Residential School… sometime in the '40's?" Pauline asked.

"You know, I heard on the news, that they closed that garbage of a school down. I believe it was in '68. I don't recall the exact date. Yes, it was in '68," said Pauline.

"Oh yea, I won't forget something as important as that either, Pauline," I replied. "Remember it was first opened around 1922. You know, when all was said and done, the children returned to their respective homes as virtual strangers… psychologically traumatized. The future generation of Native culture has been up almost uprooted. The youth returned home in an Indian body, but with a white man's mind. Today, Native communities are striving to heal from centuries of cruel and malicious intervention." I recalled.

Mrs. Ash and her family had since moved away. Nevertheless, she always treasured her visits with Mom Suse.

"Remember the fuss that took place up here in the Preston area, November of 1972?" asked Mrs. Ash.

"That commotion occurred at our Middle School," she added.

"What was the cause?" I asked.

"Oh, our students didn't receive any satisfaction until the Student Union printed their story in the school newspaper. They felt it was important to keep the community up-to-date on current affairs. I believe that about two of your great-grandchildren, were in this particular class," added Mrs. Ash.

"I guess, all of the fuss came about because our folks didn't resemble the rest of the class," I quipped.

"Sometimes, Mrs. Smith, it's really hard for our children in these new designed integrated schools. The racial discrimination is almost too painful to bear. Most times, it only serves to choke the learning process, leaving them with deep psychological scars. You see, Mrs. Smith, many of our students manage to achieve... to graduate, but the confidence to live out their dream is lacking. And looking for work, that's so difficult. Except for that ray of light at the end of the tunnel. Oh, it can be done but it will be a struggle. Some will not have enough self-confidence to handle the constant, negative pressure. How can a child survive the weeds of hate?" asked the teacher.

"Our beautiful colour has become a curse to society. But too often, self-hatred that is mirrored from the world, is reflected inward," I noted.

"Some strange, isn't it, how they lay in the sun to achieve our colour, but yet, they are quick to reject people of colour," said Mrs. Ash.

"Jealously kills!" I replied.

"Exactly," added Mrs. Ash.

"Mind ya', Mrs. Ash, our children have a great responsibility to future generations. They must avoid congregating **solely** with our own. We must make a decided **effort** to integrate. Life is full of challenges and this is the only way future generations will succeed... in this province. At first, it will be difficult, but it can be done. And in the end, it will **all** be worth it." I stated.

"Mrs. Ash, some years ago, a radio program was joking about Nova Scotia being the 14th American Colony. I know that there were 13 American Colonies. I wasn't quite sure of what to make of it," I said, totally confused.

"Mrs. Smith, the radio program was referring to the psychological and financial effect that British colonization had on Nova Scotians. This is most likely due to the fact that the Halifax was initially built as a naval and military base. You see, the province benefited in times of war because we served the needs of the British military," said the teacher.

"The needs? The good and bad?" I asked.

"All of their needs," affirmed Mrs. Ash with a twinkle in her eye.

"Oh, so the province's financial gain helped to increase the lifestyle?" I said.

"After awhile, that's all that mattered. The British sentiment ran high back then. It still runs so high that most Nova Scotians, only *wish* they were British. The whites and blacks, alike," said Mrs. Ash.

"Really? Not me, I'm just content with being Canadian," I revealed.

"Me too," added Mrs. Ash.

"You know, a little while ago, Cassius Clay spent sometime with the Muslim Leader, Malcolm X," I recalled.

"Hm, that's more than likely, since they were both Muslim. It wasn't the religion that killed Malcolm X – it was the people, back and white, alike," said Mrs. Ash

"Like I said before, 'jealously kills'!" I exclaimed.

"Mrs. Ash, why do you think that Malcolm X started out with accepting violence, when Martin Luther King, stood for peace?" I asked in bewilderment.

"Due to no fault of his own. We have to understand about Malcolm's tragic and violent childhood. We need to understand where he was coming from," replied Mrs. Ash.

"His daddy, Earl Little, was a Baptist preacher in Nebraska who heard about Marcus Garvey, the Jamaican leader. Mrs. Smith, I know that you've heard about Garvey. Well, in the 1920's, he planned to unite black people from the West Indies, America, and even here, in Nova Scotia. To be exact, two sites in Cape Breton and Halifax. His goal was to take his followers back to Africa, where they wouldn't have to suffer from the pangs of a hateful society. Now, the Little family had eight children. Malcolm's mother was a beautiful mulatto woman, whose own mother had been raped by a white man. The Little family were 100% set on supporting Garvey's vision. The only problem was that the preacher's sermons spoke on Garvey's vision of freedom. Some Klansmen got wind of this freedom talk. They threatened his family's safety by fire-bombing their house," recalled Mrs. Ash.

Vivian Willis

The teacher took a short pause.

"Mrs. Ash, It's all so cruel, so, so unnecessary," I said.

The teacher continued, "Everyone was awakened... Thank God, there were no injuries. Eventually though, the clan attacked the Preacher outside one night and threw his badly beaten body on the streetcar tracks. He was bashed around the head, but still very much alive," added Mrs. Ash.

I sniffled, a bit. I felt as though, I could see his battered face.

"Not long after the murder of her husband, Mrs. Little, was sent to an asylum," added Mrs. Ash.

"Say what? An asylum. Why? What else happened?" I asked

"First, the insurance company, told her that, "benefits were not paid out for suicide deaths". And then, the Children's Aid sent a Social Worker to torture the poor widow. The worker warned that, "her children would end up as delinquents and be sent to reform schools. Malcolm was only eight when his father was murdered. He was an eight-year old orphan. He grew up in reform schools. His traumatic childhood did nothing for his self-worth. While in the orphanage, a teacher discouraged him from pursuing a career law. Malcom was a brilliant student with a brilliant mind. Instead, he was advised to find a trade focusing on manual labour," recalled Mrs. Ash.

"Minus parental love and guidance, Malcolm followed a life of crime. Eventually, he was jailed a few times. This was where he met the Muslim brother who steered him in the right direction," added Mrs. Ash.

"I can see why he grew up to despise white folk; they didn't leave him with much of a choice. In fact, they didn't leave him with anything... and only eight years old. Um, um, um," I said.

"True, but in the end, Malcolm learned to love the human race, whites included," recalled Mrs. Ash.

"Now, on the other hand, the childhood of Martin Luther King was altogether different. King also grew up being surrounded by a loving Christian family. However, the KKK never attacked, threatened or hounded the King family," commented Mrs. Ash.

"When all was said and done, they were both gunned down - in the prime of life. What a shame, shame, shame!" I stated.

"Um, um, um," added the teacher.

In 1983, the Black Cultural Centre of Nova Scotia was founded. This multifaceted centre was the brainchild of the late Dr. W.P. Oliver, a prominent Baptist Minister, and a recipient of the Order of Canada.

The building is situated on Hwy #7 at entrance of the Preston area communities, and across the street from the Home for Coloured Children.

The Centre contains a museum, an auditorium, library, educational resource facilities, tour guide arrangements and much more.

Chapter 17

Over her illustrious years, Mom Suse imparted many words of wisdom to her children and grandchildren. Her one hundred plus years had led her through countless experiences, too numerous to mention. Mom Suse found many solutions to life's trials and tribulations from first-hand experiences. This granddame genuinely cared a great deal about the welfare of others, in that, she was always prepared to lend an ear and a helping hand to anyone, regardless of race, creed, religion, or economic status. The unselfish love that she shared with others was always a source of solace to them.

Vivian Willis, one of Mom Suse's granddaughters, has many beautiful memories of the times in which she spent at Mom Suse's side. Their cheerful, uplifting conversations were truly inspirational. Vivian will never forget how much her grandmother set her on the straight and narrow, and kept here there.

"There's goodness in so many people in the world," I said. "You should always show your best side to them, dear, and hopefully, with God's help, they'll show you their best side."

"That's a beautiful thought!" said Vivian. "I'll sure try to live up to that motto."

"I hope so dear," I said. "Because when you do, you're showing your best side to God too!"

"I'll have to remember that," said Vivian. "It's difficult sometimes to be that way, but I think that's the way I'd like to be!"

"I hope so Vivian, because when I'm gone, having that kind of treasure in your heart will always keep you safe from harm!" I commented.

"I'm really fortunate to have you for a granny!" commented Vivian, totally overjoyed at her grandmother's insight. "I'll do my best to live up to these high standards – I really will!" Vivian exclaimed.

"I'm sure you will, dear, I'm sure you will. But you have to remember to share this wisdom with others so they can have a good life, too!" I said, encouragingly.

"I'll make sure that my children and any others who want to listen, will get the benefit of what you've told me," said Vivian. "That way, all the good you've done for me will go on and on!"

"I feel very fortune to have a granddaughter like you, Vivian," I said. "Not everyone cares about us old people the way that you do. I hope that when you get to be my age and have grandchildren, they are as good to you, as you have been to me," I added, gratefully.

"I sure hope so too, Granny!" said Vivian as she gave me a big hug and kiss.

"Well, my dear, I hope you'll always have a love for God. Believe you me, that's the most important decision you will have to make," I stated.

"When you live by that motto. I think that the rest will take care of itself. I don't mean to put myself as high as God – in no way do I mean that. But when you have the love of God, as well as your family then you are on a strong path of righteousness, that is hard for bad people to get you off!" I stated.

"I've always felt a strong attachment to my family," said Vivian, "but you're right. If we put God and family first – the rest will really take care of itself."

"I can see that my words are sewn in fertile ground," I said. "I'm glad we were able to talk like this, because it's very important that someone who really cares about me and what I say, is someone who will pass on my thoughts on life and share them with others," I noted.

"Granny, if I ever live to be your age. I want to be just like you!" said Vivian, with much love and conviction. She gave me a gentle hug.

Granny Suse was nearing her 103rd birthday. Vivian was glad to have the occasion to bath her. As usual, she asked me to make her real clean.

Vivian Willis

"Wash me good, now, because men like it when a woman is real clean," she would often comment.

"Another thing, Vivian - be sure to cream my body real good, now. It's not right for a woman to walk around with scruffy heels and ashy skin," Granny reminded me.

We both had a good laugh. It was comforting to be back in the company of Granny Suse.

"Granny, you wouldn't have any trouble remembering the olden days, would you?" I asked.

"What is it young lady? My body may be feeble, but my mind is as sharp as a tack," I replied. "Don't by shy, ask away!"

"Well, during the construction of the old Macdonald Bridge, I understand that the land under the bridge was undisturbed on both sides of the harbour. They didn't tear down a single house or move a single soul. Yet, in building the new A. Murray MacKay Bridge, the land on Dartmouth's Turtle's Cove, the old Native Burial Grounds were destroyed. And in Halifax everybody knows what happened to the black community of Africville, 'near death by bulldozer'! Granny, those people are really crazy! How can the dead rest in peace when their remains and community aren't respected?" Vivian questioned.

"My dear young lady, those dear departed will continue to rest in peace, but I'm certain, the same can't be said for the destroyers of a sacred burial ground and community. Some things should **never** be touched. But don't worry none, 'cause everyone must deal with their **own** conscience before we depart this old world," I answered.

"Sometime ago I heard that our Preston men helped to build this city of Halifax and Dartmouth. It that right?" quizzed Vivian.

"If the true be told, these cities belong to you, as much as it does to the white folk, or anyone else. First of all, this **here** is God's ground! It's meant for all people to applaud our oneness, and respect our differences. Honey, our Preston ancestors were very much responsible for building the core of our cities; bridges included. And don't you forget it." I replied, emphatically.

March 10, 1986, was a great day for a celebration. Mom Suse was one hundred and three years old. It was always a magnificent Smith family reunion. Her illustrious life deserves respect. Many from her large family would make their presence known by sending cards, flowers or extending personal greetings to the woman who touched their lives.

For some, her generosity was a catapult for their success. On Mom Suse's birthday, they would respond by making impromptu appearances, knowing full well that they were always welcomed at the Smith home. A head count was taken when the Smith clan had all arrived. It just about took one's breath away.

At age 103, Mom Suse was the matriarch of eight children, eighty-four grandchildren, three hundred forty-six great grandchildren, two hundred thirty-two great, great grandchildren, and seven great, great, great grandchildren.

This birthday was a truly memorable experience. The CBC (Canadian Broadcasting Corporation) wrote and broadcasted a one-hour documentary on her life. The interview proceeded as Mom Suse would have wished, relaxed and informal. The show feature Mom Suse's reflections and anecdotes from a long and fruitful life, including her friends and relatives who gathered for moral support. When the interview was completed, the crew bid Mom Suse farewell and packed away their gear - in order for Mom Suse to enjoy the day with family and friends. True to her nature, Mom Suse would not let the CBC crew off the hook, until they had enjoyed a slice of birthday cake and some beverages. When all was said and done, the crew was surprised to find that they were treated just like family.

One of Mom Suse's daughters, asked the camera operators, if they would be so kind as to film the upcoming special at the community church service in Mom Suse's honour. The crew readily agreed to accept.

But first, the gifts had to be unwrapped. One present, in particular, stood out from the rest. It was given by grandson Dennis and his wife Ollie. Mom Suse unwrapped the heaviest of boxes and produced a brand new fur coat. Trying hard to suppress the laughter that was soon to bubble over, Mom Suse asked.

"Where'd you get that 'old thing' from?" Then she proceeded to say, "A young woman such as myself needs something stylish, not reliable. And that they ought to return it to the poor animal they took it from so it could return to the forest."

Everyone laughed. Well, Mom Suse laughed so hard that she almost toppled off the chair. Following the gift opening, the CBC crew accompanied the Smith family to the small community church. Talented like her dear, departed father, Leota, the youngest daughter, provided the music.

Reverend Donald Skeir approached the podium.

"Ladies, gentlemen and children, I do not have to tell you why we are here today, but I will, anyways. We are all in attendance to pay homage to this lovely young lady in the front pew whom we hold near and dear to our hearts. This lady is a legend in her time! In fact, I guarantee that many of you here have a special story of your own. It is certain, that you can attest to this remarkable fact. Our lovely choir will perform the next few songs. In essence, they contain the very heart and soul of sweet inspiration.

The music is sure to capture the spirit of this grateful day. By the way, the choir members are relatives of Mom Suse, except for one. The Negro spiritual that she holds very dear is, 'Swing Low Sweet Chariot'. After that spirit-filled rendition, the choir's angelic sang out with, 'Amazing Grace'."

Reverend Skeir continued.

"My dear friends, I feel that these songs have captured the sentiment of the day, contained in their essence, the heart and soul of the sweet inspiration we have felt from knowing Mom Suse. I have known this woman since I was a young boy, and my sermons have frequently been inspired by the words of wisdom that she has shared with me," he continued.

"Although many kind comments can be said of Mom Suse, there was a time she was cursed and degraded by ignorant people. Some even called her the 'Witch of North Preston'. I know for a fact, that some of our older deacons of previous decades, indicated as much, in no subtle words or deeds, toward both her and her family. Today, we are honouring this saintly woman. However, I believe that today is her day of vindication for all of the cruel and vicious things that have been said about her. I now end these wonderful words of adulation to our dear friend, Susannah Bundy Smith. The choir will sing a favourite hymn of her dear, departed husband, Demus, who was the chief organist of our church for over fifty years, "I Don't Have to Cry No More, When Jesus Comes," concluded Reverend Skeir.

The minister invited Mom Suse to say few words. Her speech was short and sweet.

"I want to thank you all for coming here today. All I want to say is put your faith in God. When you are depressed and feel there is no hope. He will be there for you. When you live by that motto, I think the rest will take care of itself. I don't mean to put myself as high as God, but when you have the love of God, as well as the love of your family, then you are on a strong path of righteousness that even bad people cannot rid themselves of you," she stated.

The CBC network was able to capture this memorable event, documented on the life of the granddame, herself, Mom Suse. The documentary was so well received by the Canadian viewing audience, the CBC crew returned to North Preston the following year to film a sequel on Mom Suse's life, thereby, delving further into the soul of this unique woman. The wisdom, presence and astounding longevity of Mom Suse will be remembered.

As time had allowed, Vivian would travel back home to Nova Scotia, in order to, spend quality-time with her centenarian grandmother. Vivian sought out, yet a greater appreciation of Mom Suse's lifetime of love and sacrifice. On one occasion, Vivian brought a newspaper article contrasting the difference in the cost of living from 1923 to 1987, a sixty-four year span.

"Granny, look at this, a loaf of bread. In 1923 it cost only .07¢, but this year were paying $1.38, that's ridiculous," said Vivian.

"Does it mention the price of milk?" I asked.

"Actually, it does Granny. Back in your day, a gallon of milk was .47¢. Now were paying up to $3.99 a gallon. The next item is butter. It used to be .46¢ a pound. Today, it costs us $2.81 a pound. The gas prices were as low as .28¢. Not so now, we have to fork out $1.69 a gallon.

"I've only got two more items to go Granny, in case this is boring you," said Vivian, thoughtfully.

"No dear, not at all. I think this is a good idea, then you can see, in some ways, how life has gotten harder and not easier," I said.

"At least on the pocketbook," I added.

Vivian Willis

"Okay Granny, now where was I? Oh, yes. In 1923, the price of a new house sold for $2,582.00. You won't believe this, today's price tag is asking for $86,079.00," said Vivian, despairingly. "The last item has to do with personal income. In the olden days a person made an average of $1,090.00 a year, but that average has now soared to $21,737.00," commented Vivian.

"Vivian, give me the difference on the individual items, and we'll be able to see how the economy has been choking the life out of people," I said.

"Sure Granny, no problem. Today, we pay more than $1.31 for a loaf of bread, and $3.52 extra for a gallon of milk. For a pound of butter, it costs $2.35 more and the price of gas has risen to $1.41 extra. Get this Granny," exclaimed Vivian.

"The soaring cost of a house, is now more than $8,349.97.00. The last item is personal income. Today, we take home more than $20,647.00 each year," reported Vivian.

"Um, but the high cost of living eats it all up. It seems to be getting more and more difficult for people to make ends meet, especially the poor. Yes, nowadays, you fellas have more freedom, opportunities, education than we did, but the financial pressure just about puts you, right in the 'dog house'", I said.

"In the good old days, we would struggle, but nothing like how you fellas have to struggle. One whole dollar, would go a long way, back then." I added. "In that regard, it was a gentler time."

"I guess that's why they called it the 'good old days," said Vivian. "Life was not as financially pressured."

"Um hm," I agreed.

In 1880, the telephone service in both City of Halifax and Town of Dartmouth was created in business establishments. Public Telephones were installed on street corners. The fee for its use ranged from 5 to 10 cents.

In the late 1890's, the City of Halifax and the Town of Dartmouth received electric light and power service. As well, Halifax and Dartmouth established electrical streetcar operation around the turn of the century.

By late 1950's the black community of New Road, received light and power. This service was, at first, initiated to the major service structures such as the streetlights, the church, the schoolhouse and the community store.

Telephone services were installed in the community of North Preston around the late 1960's. During that decade, the use of horse and buggies (wagon) would eventually be weeded out for public transportation. But, more so, in the mid '50's since the advent of the Macdonald Bridge. The automobile had become fashionable and much more feasible.

In the '70's, the community was serviced with door-to-door milk delivery. However, our folk travelled to Dartmouth for mail picked-up at the Main Postal Station. The new A. Murray MacKay Bridge connecting Halifax to Dartmouth opened in July of 1970.

As mentioned earlier, Mom Suse's birthdays were full of celebrated surprises. Her one hundred and fifth was no exception. Unbeknownst to the granddame, herself, her granddaughter, Vivian Willis, had an incredible surprise planned. Six months earlier, Vivian had started the wheels in motion.

She mailed a copy of Mom Suse's birth certificate and forwarded it to Parliament Hill, Ottawa. Once a copy of a Birth Certificate as been sent, the Canadian government provides certificates in honour of birthdays of 65 years and over with a message from the Prime Minister. Any birthdays of 90 years and over would receive a message from the Governor General.

A citizen celebrating a birthday of 100 years or more, and every fifth year, thereafter, would look forward to receiving a message from her Majesty, Queen Elizabeth II.

Then came the expected red tape, and Vivian was on the phone to Ottawa almost daily. It seemed that her carefully made plans would fall through and the awaited document would not arrive on time.

She was promised that the surprise would be delivered promptly and personally on March 10th, 1988. On the morning of her grandmother's birthday, the morning had arrived along with the awaited surprise.

On that morning, Mom Suse was enjoying a cup of tea with her daughter, Ruth, when they heard a knock on the front door. It was too early for the celebrations to begin the family and friends weren't expected until the afternoon.

Of course, Ruth was in on the secret, but acted as if she didn't have a clue as to who was at the door. At that time, Ruth exchanged quizzical glances with her mother before rising to end the suspense.

Actually, Ruth was struck with a combination of astonishment and curiosity, even though she had known what to expect. The Premier of Nova Scotia, The Honourable John Buchanan, himself, stood on their doorstep holding a large bouquet of flowers.

"Hello, I have come here to wish Susannah Smith a happy 105th birthday and to present her with these," the Premiere glanced at the gorgeous bouquet he was holding.

"Come in, won't you?" asked Ruth, equally polite. She led the premier into the parlour.

"Mom", Ruth smiled as she entered, "the Premier of Nova Scotia is here, to see you."

"The Premier, himself, Mr. John Buchanan, is here to see me?" I asked in awe. "Oh, well tell him to come right on in. Mr. Premier, please have a seat," I said, rather brightly. "I feel very honoured by your visit."

"Nonsense, it is I who should have the honour," said the Premier.

"You're a very special person, having such an extraordinarily long and fruitful life. And for this very special occasion, I bring you flowers and personal greetings from the Prime Minister of Canada, The Honourable, Brian Mulroney."

"Again, the honour is mine. Thank you very much and be sure to give my regards to our Prime Minister," I said.

"You are a very gracious lady," said the Premier. As he presented me with a bouquet of flowers, he bent down and graciously kissed me on the cheek.

He stayed long enough to enjoy a cup of tea with the granddame. The atmosphere was filled with honour and respect.

A short while later, there was another knock on the door. This time is was a postal worker.

"I have a special delivery letter for Susannah Smith," he said unable to hide his excitement. "It's from the Queen of England herself."

Ruth was beside herself with appreciation. "Open it up Mom, it's from Queen Elizabeth II, of England."

"Open it for me, dear and read what it says," I asked nonchalantly.

"It really is from the Queen, Mom," said Ruth after scanning the contents. "She is formally congratulating you on your one hundred and fifth birthday! And there's something else, here... hey Mom, here is a certificate to prove it."

"That's really nice dear. Will you please hand me my glasses so I can read?" I asked.

"The Queen has some really nice things to say about me," I said.

"I really do feel special today."

"To me, you are special every day. You are the most special person in the world to me," she said affectionately, as she bent down and gave me a big hug and kiss. "Happy Birthday, Mom." said Ruth.

It was the year 1988, and Vivian, wanted to commemorate her grandmother's one hundred and fifth birthday in a unique way. Especially since Vivian had moved away from the East Coast, many years before.

After much deliberation, she decided to name a star after Mom Suse. It would be a fitting tribute to the wonderful matriarch. As fortune would have it, Vivian was introduced to Ivan, an astronomer at a party. It was the perfect place and time to seek out her much needed information.

"Is it possible to have a star named after my Granny?" Vivian asked. "She just turned 105, and I want to show her how special she is."

"I don't foresee a problem with that," said Ivan. "Why stop there? I can have stars named after other people who are dear to your heart."

"That would be fabulous," said Vivian. "I've always wanted to have a star named after my daughter, Solea and my mother, Pauline."

Ivan smiled. That shouldn't be a problem."

"I don't want to rush you, but my Granny is not in perfect health, and she might not be around much longer. I would like to get it done, as soon as possible," commented Vivian.

"I'll start working on it, right away," Ivan said eagerly. "Once everything is finalized, I'll send the official certificates indicating the stars that have been named after your three special people."

"Thanks for all of the help, Ivan," said Vivian, gratefully, as she and Ivan parted company. "I'm looking forward to hearing from you!"

As time went by, Vivian was beginning to become quite concerned with the health of Mom Suse. It was for this reason that Vivian began to call her Aunt Ruth daily for an update on the health of her grandmother.

After about two weeks, the official certificates regarding the star naming had finally arrived. There was a Special Delivery to Vivian's house in the Scarborough Bluffs area of Toronto. Vivian accepted the envelope before heading off to work.

"It's the certificates!" said an elated Vivian to herself.

"I must phone Aunt Ruth so she can let Granny know that they've arrived. She'll be so happy," said Vivian proudly.

"Hi! Aunt Ruth? This is Vivian. Do you remember when I told you that I was going to have a star named after Granny, one of my daughters, Solea and my Mom? Well the certificates have finally arrived! Will you please tell Granny when you see her today, at the hospital?" asked Vivian.

"I sure will, Vivian," said her Aunt Ruth. "She'll be so glad to hear it. She's been looking forward to it ever since you told about your plans for her. Thanks for calling. Bye Vivian, God Bless," said Aunt Ruth.

"Bye, Aunt Ruth! Give my love to Granny! Vivian said.

After a full day's work, Vivian arrived home at one a.m., the following day. She was home only a short time when the phone call came from Aunt Ruth.

"Hello, Vivian. I have some bad news for you, so I think that you should sit down. Your dear, beloved Granny had passed away, about an hour ago."

Vivian's thought process was in suspension. She paused and couldn't quite get her mind around what she had heard and seemed to be paralyzed with shock.

"Oh, no! I can't believe it!" said Vivian. Although she half-expected to hear these words, the reality left her with a comfortless cold chill.

In recognition of Mom Suses, the CBC aired the documentary of Mom Suse's 103rd Birthday, on Christmas of 1988.

In the spring of 1986, one of Mom Suse's grandsons, Joel Willis, was fatally wounded while coming to the rescue one of his brothers.

Joel believed in the protection of family, he gave the ultimate… he gave his life. His epitaph reads as thus.

> There's an open gate at the end of the road
> Through which we all must go alone
> In addition, there is a light we cannot see
> Our Father claims his own
> Beyond the gates your loved one
> Find happiness and rest
> And there is comfort in the thought
> That a loving God knows best.

At the church service for the Late Susannah Bundy Smith, Reverend Donald Skeir gave a heart-felt eulogy.

"Susannah Smith leaves a legacy for all to follow. She shares the podium along with other great men and women of Nova Scotia. They strove to build a better life for their descendants, by overcoming the obstacles without loosing hope. Mom Suse was able to kiss the clouds, yet remain humble and unaffected by tribulations. There are too many people in this world, who mouth the words of a pious man on Sunday, then flout His word the other six days. The dedication of this saintly woman revealed itself daily in possessing her soul toward our Lord Jesus Christ. Mom Suse fervently believed that people were placed on this blessed earth for the benefit of each other. She strove to make the world a better place. These scruples caused her to stand out in a world filled with much greed and intolerance. Although she battled the narrow mindedness of others, throughout her life, she never considered being black a disadvantage. She forged a trail so that others could follow and have an easier time of it. In the sea of despair, it was that same strength that allowed her to keep not only

Vivian Willis

her family's head above water, but kept others from drowning. The generosity that the Good Lord bestowed upon her, she readily shared with folks in the Preston area communities and beyond. It is a known fact that Mom Suse gave far more to her community, than she ever received. 'Always working – never resting,' could well have been her personal motto. Remember to take heed of the actions and intentions of this grand woman. Our Lord graced the earth with her soul and kindred spirit for a reason, to show that it is not in the possession of material objects that makes the person, but in the depth of the soul. This world would have been an insufferable place in which to live, without the depth of love, and strength of grace from Mom Suse. May we each strive, by the grace of God, to emulate, even a degree of her life!"

APPENDIX

Turn of the Century Clothing

Ladies' undergarments (corsets & petticoat))

Ladies 2 piece suit complete with wide brim hat & umbrella

Styles that Will Be Much Worn
Peerless Patterns   Ten Cents Each

4711. LADIES' TUCKED SHIRT-WAIST.   4717. LADIES' YOKE SHIRT-WAIST.

Ladies' Fine Honeycomb Wool Shawl

Seal Grain Leather Shopping Bag

Ladies' Silk Lined Cashmere Gloves

Ladies Shirt-Waist, Wool Shawl, Leather Shopping Bag and Cashmere Gloves

Girls' dresses, girls' box-coat & child's full-length apron

Boy's waterproof 2 piece suit

Boys' or Misses Rain Coat

Furniture, carpets, stoves etc.

MAPS

MAP ONE: MI'KMAKI (Mi'kmaq Homeland)

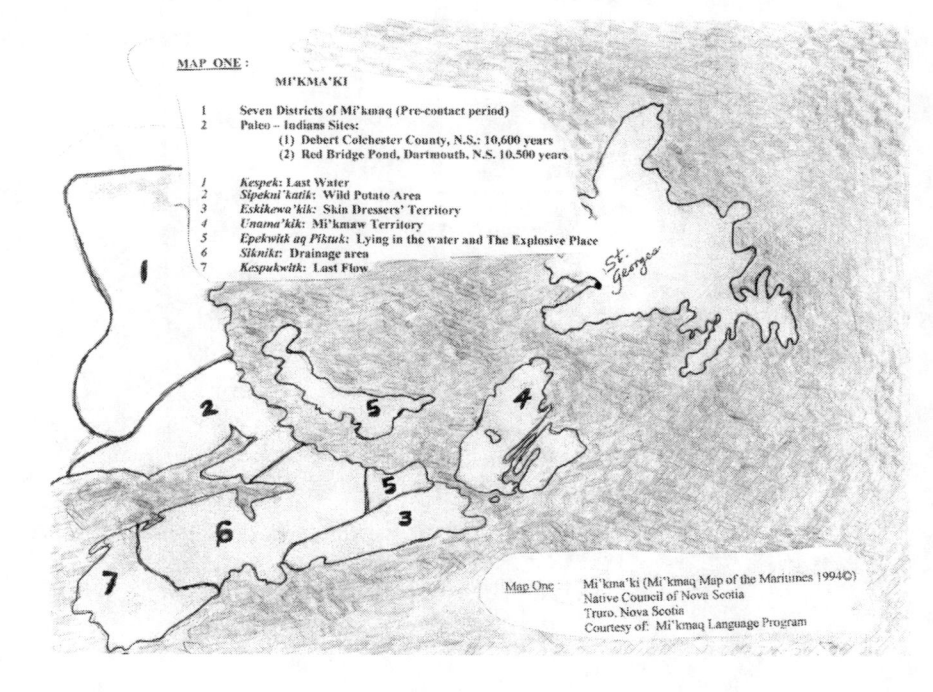

MAP ONE:
MI'KMA'KI

1   Seven Districts of Mi'kmaq (Pre-contact period)
2   Paleo – Indians Sites:
        (1) Debert Colchester County, N.S.: 10,600 years
        (2) Red Bridge Pond, Dartmouth, N.S. 10,500 years

1   *Kespek*: Last Water
2   *Sipekni'katik*: Wild Potato Area
3   *Eskikewa'kik*: Skin Dressers' Territory
4   *Unama'kik*: Mi'kmaw Territory
5   *Epekwitk aq Piktuk*: Lying in the water and The Explosive Place
6   *Sikniki*: Drainage area
7   *Kespukwitk*: Last Flow

Map One: Mi'kma'ki (Mi'kmaq Map of the Maritimes 1994©)
Native Council of Nova Scotia
Truro, Nova Scotia
Courtesy of: Mi'kmaq Language Program

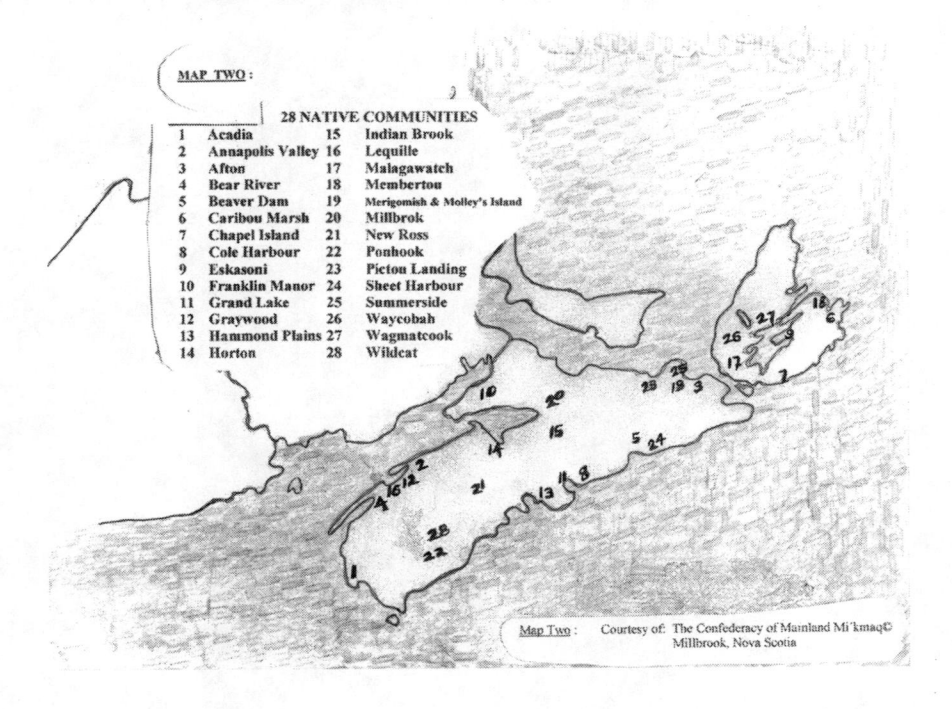

MAP TWO: 28 NATIVE COMMUNITIES

MAP TWO:

28 NATIVE COMMUNITIES

1	Acadia	15	Indian Brook
2	Annapolis Valley	16	Lequille
3	Afton	17	Malagawatch
4	Bear River	18	Membertou
5	Beaver Dam	19	Merigomish & Molley's Island
6	Caribou Marsh	20	Millbrok
7	Chapel Island	21	New Ross
8	Cole Harbour	22	Ponhook
9	Eskasoni	23	Picton Landing
10	Franklin Manor	24	Sheet Harbour
11	Grand Lake	25	Summerside
12	Graywood	26	Waycobah
13	Hammond Plains	27	Wagmatcook
14	Horton	28	Wildcat

Map Two: Courtesy of: The Confederacy of Mainland Mi'kmaq©
Millbrook, Nova Scotia

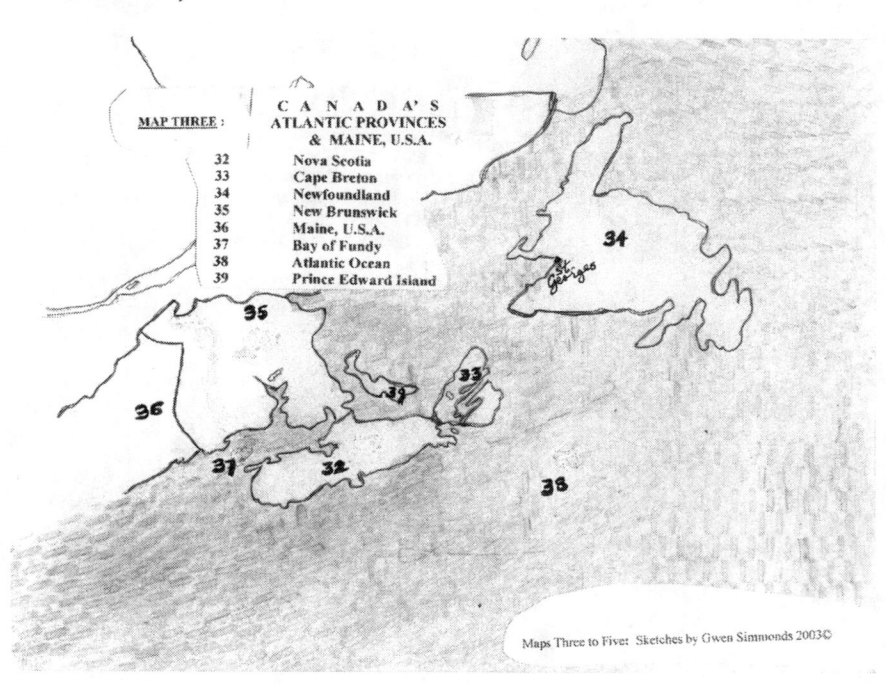

MAP THREE: CANADA'S ATLANTIC PROVINCES & MAINE, U.S.A.

MAP THREE:
CANADA'S
ATLANTIC PROVINCES
& MAINE, U.S.A.
32 Nova Scotia
33 Cape Breton
34 Newfoundland
35 New Brunswick
36 Maine, U.S.A.
37 Bay of Fundy
38 Atlantic Ocean
39 Prince Edward Island

Maps Three to Five: Sketches by Gwen Simmonds 2003©

MAP FOUR: HALIFAX HARBOUR

MAP FOUR:

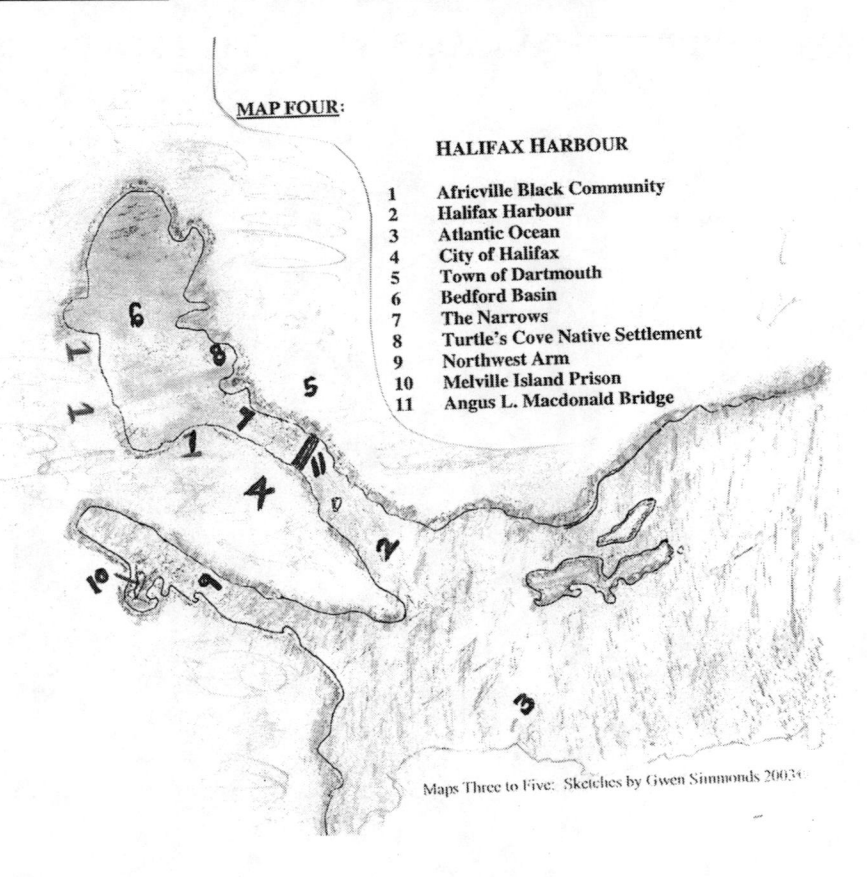

HALIFAX HARBOUR

1. Africville Black Community
2. Halifax Harbour
3. Atlantic Ocean
4. City of Halifax
5. Town of Dartmouth
6. Bedford Basin
7. The Narrows
8. Turtle's Cove Native Settlement
9. Northwest Arm
10. Melville Island Prison
11. Angus L. Macdonald Bridge

Maps Three to Five: Sketches by Gwen Simmonds 2003

MAP FIVE: PRESTON AREA BLACK COMMUNITIES

MAP FIVE:

PRESTON AREA COMMUNITIES

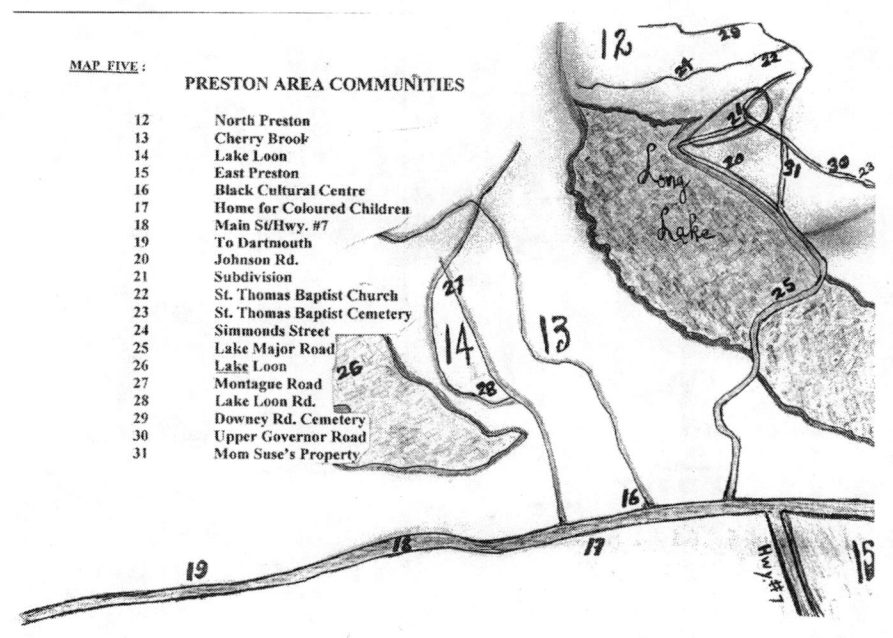

12	North Preston
13	Cherry Brook
14	Lake Loon
15	East Preston
16	Black Cultural Centre
17	Home for Coloured Children
18	Main St/Hwy. #7
19	To Dartmouth
20	Johnson Rd.
21	Subdivision
22	St. Thomas Baptist Church
23	St. Thomas Baptist Cemetery
24	Simmonds Street
25	Lake Major Road
26	Lake Loon
27	Montague Road
28	Lake Loon Rd.
29	Downey Rd. Cemetery
30	Upper Governor Road
31	Mom Suse's Property

Maps Three to Five: Sketches by Gwen Simmonds 2003©

MAP SIX: 48 BLACK COMMUNITIES

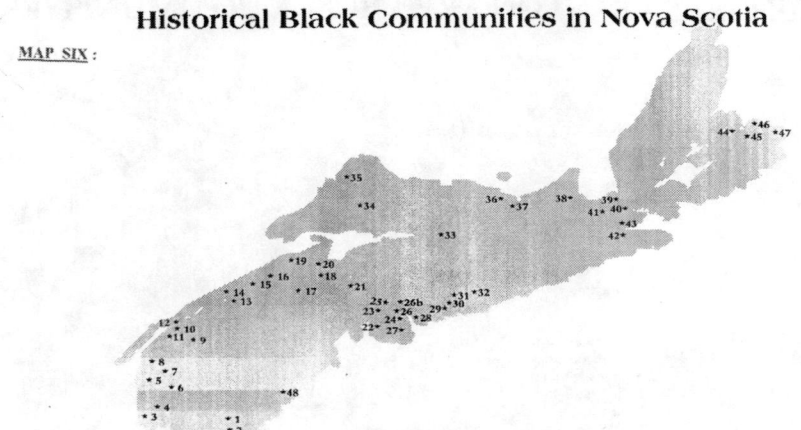

Historical Black Communities in Nova Scotia

MAP SIX :

SHELBURNE
1 - Shelburne
2 - Birchtown

YARMOUTH
3 - Yarmouth
4 - Greenville

ANNAPOLIS
13 - LeQuille
14 - Granville Ferry
15 - Inglewood (Bridgetown)
16 - Middleton

KINGS
17 - Cambridge
18 - Gibson Woods
19 - Aldershot
20 - Kentville

DIGBY
5 - Southville
6 - Danvers
7 - Hassett
8 - Weymouth Falls
9 - Jordantown
10 - Conway
11 - Acaciaville
12 - Digby

QUEENS
48 - Liverpool

HANTS
21 - Three Miles Plains

HALIFAX
22 - Beechville
23 - Hammonds Plains
24 - Africville
25 - Lucasville
26 - Cobequid Road
26B - Maroon Hill
27 - Halifax
28 - Dartmouth
29 - Lake Loon
30 - Cherry Brook
31 - North Preston
32 - East Preston

COLCHESTER
33 - Truro

CUMBERLAND
34 - Springhill
35 - Amherst

PICTOU
36 - Trenton
37 - New Glasgow

ANTIGONISH
38 - Antigonish
39 - Monastery

GUYSBOROUGH
40 - Mulgrave
41 - Upper Big Tracadie
42 - Lincolnville
43 - Sunnyville

CAPE BRETON
44 - North Sydney
45 - Sydney
46 - New Waterford
47 - Glace Bay
Specific rural black communities in Nova Scotoia

Map Six : Courtesy of : The Black Culture Centre©
Westphal, Nova Scotia, Canada

MAP ONE: MI'KMA'KI

1. Seven Districts of Mi'kmaq (Pre-contact period)
2. Paleo – Indians Sites:
   (i) Debert Colchester County, N.S.: 10,600 years
   (ii) Red Bridge Pond, Dartmouth, N.S.: 10,500 years

1. *Kespek*: Last Water
2. *Sipekni'katik*: Wild Potato Area
3. *Eskikewa'kik*: Skin Dressers' Territory
4. *Unama'kik:* Mi'kmaw Territory
5. *Epekwitk aq Piktuk:* Lying in the water and The Exposive Place
6. *Siknikt:* Drainage area
7. *Kespukwitk:* Last Flow

MAP TWO: 28 NATIVE COMMUNITIES

1	Acadia	15	Indian Brook
2	Annapolis Valley	16	Lequille
3	Afton	17	Malagawatch
4	Bear River	18	Membertou
5	Beaver Dam	19	Merigomish & Molley's Island
6	Caribou March	20	Millbrook
7	Chapel Island	21	New Ross
8	Cole Harbour	22	Ponhook
9	Eskasoni	23	Pictou Landing
10	Franklin Manor	24	Sheet Harbour
11	Grand Lake	25	Summerside
12	Graywood	26	Waycobah
13	Hammond Plains	27	Wagmatcook
14	Horton	28	Wildcat

MAP THREE: CANADA'S ATLANTIC PROVINCES & MAINE, U.S.A.

32   Nova Scotia
33   Cape Breton, Nova Scotia
34   Newfoundland
35   New Brunswick
36   Maine, U.S.A.
37   Bay of Fundy
38   Atlantic Ocean
39   Prince Edward Island

MAP FOUR: HALIFAX HARBOUR

1   Africville Black Community
2   Halifax Harbour
3   Atlantic Ocean
4   City of Halifax
5   Town of Dartmouth
6   Bedford Basin
7   The Narrows
8   Turtle's Cove
9   Northwest Arm
10   Melville Island Prison
11   Angus L. Macdonald Bridge

MAP FIVE: PRESTON AREA BLACK COMMUNITIES

12   North Preston
13   Cherry Brook
14   Lake Loon
15   East Preston
16   Black Cultural Centre for Nova Scotia
17   Home for Coloured Children
18   Main Street / Hwy. #7
19   To Dartmouth
20   Johnson Road
21   Subdivision
22   St. Thomas United Baptist Church
23   St. Thomas Cemetery
24   Simmonds Street
25   Lake Major Road
26   Lake Loon
27   Montague Road
28   Downey Road Cemetery
29   Upper Governor Road
30   Mom Suse's Property

MAP SIX: 48 BLACK COMMUNITIES

Note: The community names are written on the bottom of this map.

PHOTOGRAPHS

Photographs A: Courtesy of *Back in Time Photos*, Halifax, Nova Scotia

Military Prison, Melville Island, Halifax, N.S.

1800's Melville Island Prison, Northwest Arm, Halifax, N.S.

1898 Wedding in Dartmouth: Richard Tynes & Mary Ann Borden

1900 Dartmouth / Halifax Ferry Service, the Sir Charles Ogle

1900 Public Gardens, Halifax, Nova Scotia

1910 Dartmouth Ferry Terminal with Approaches

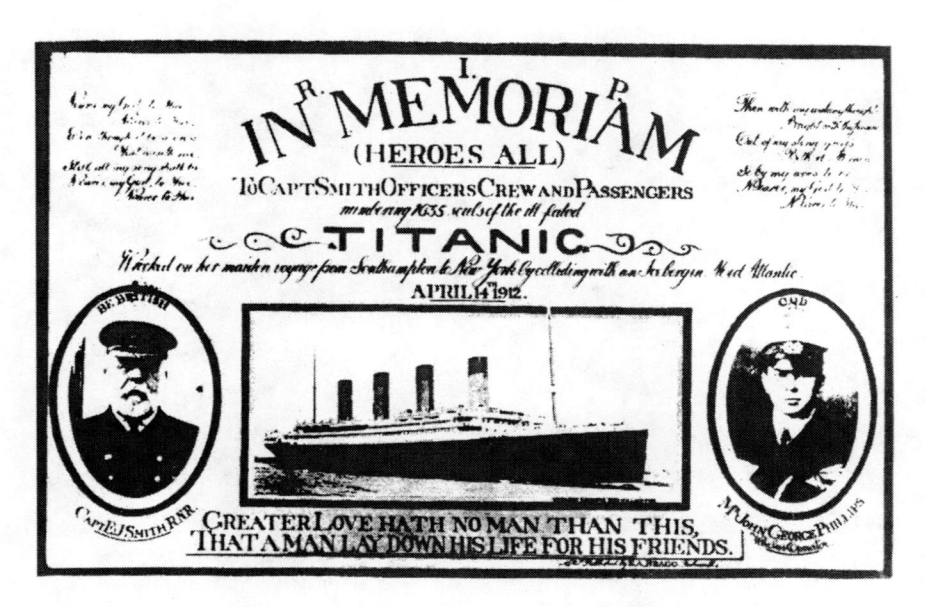

In Memoriam: *The Titanic*, April 14th, 1912

View of 'The Imo', *Halifax Explosion*, December 6th, 1917

1927 Citadel Hill Park, Halifax, Nova Scotia

1929 Aerial of Halifax Harbour and Dartmouth waterfront

1934 Streetcar and Automobiles, Barrington Street, Halifax

circa 1955-1958: Angus L. Macdonald Bridge at completion viewing Halifax's waterfront under the Dartmouth side

Photographs B: 1b–3b: Courtesy of the *Black Cultural Centre of Nova Scotia*

St. Thomas United Baptist Church, North Preston, Nova Scotia

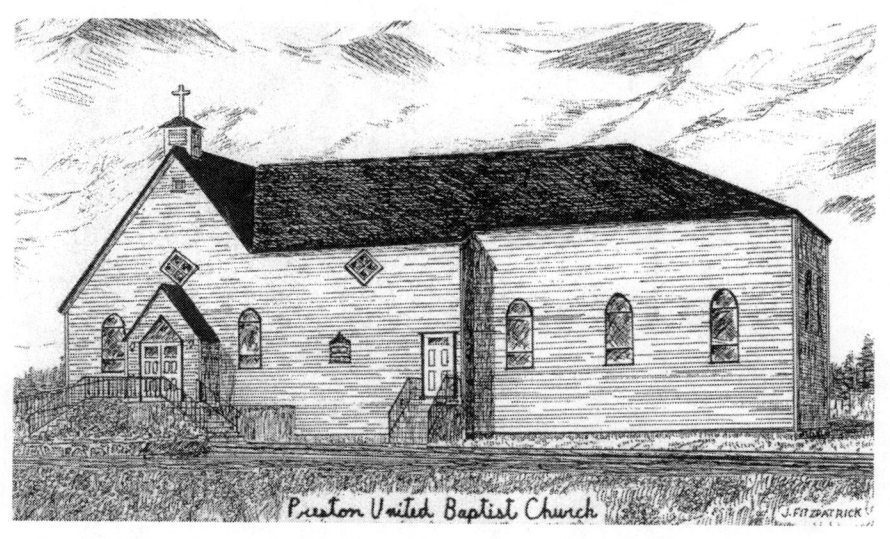

East Preston United Baptist Church, East Preston, Nova Scotia

Cherry Brook United Baptist Church, Cherry Brook, Nova Scotia

Photograph B: 4b: Courtesy of *Frank Stanley Boyd Jr.*

Cornwallis Street United Baptist, Halifax, Nova Scotia

Photographs B: 5b–8b: Courtesy of the *Black Cultural Centre of Nova Scotia*

Africville's Seaview Baptist Church 1849-1967

Seaview Park (formerly Campbell Road) United Baptist Church, Africville, Nova Scotia

Mom Suse & Wayne Adams

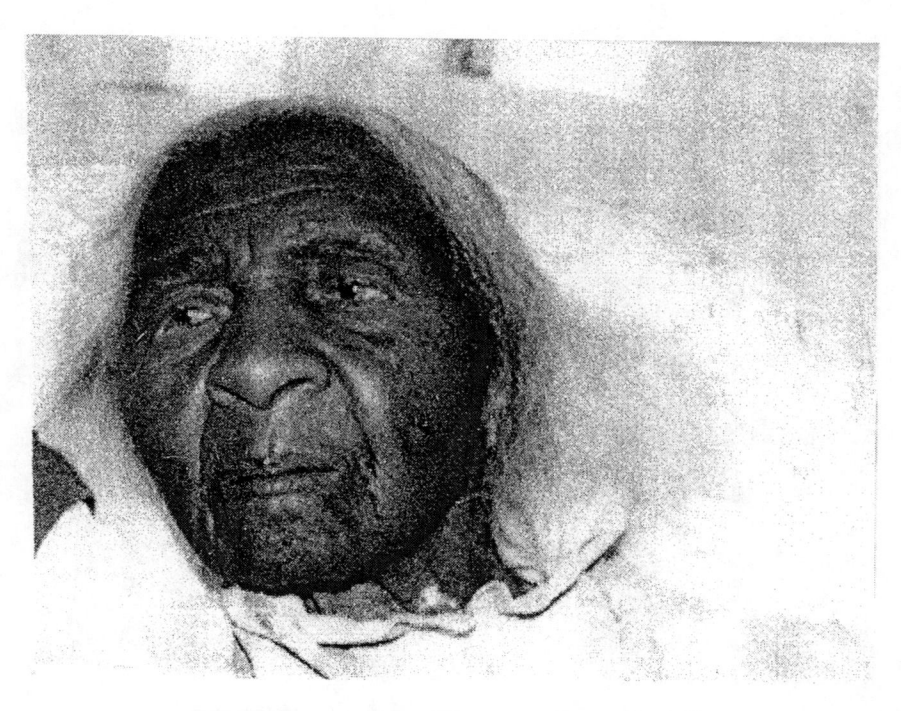

Mom Suse at age 102 years (cover page)

BLACK CULTURAL CENTRE
FOR
NOVA SCOTIA
(A Museum, Library and Auditorium Complex)

Museum
- Photographs and Paintings
- Valuables and Collectables
- Antiques and Artifacts
- Mementoes and Memorabilia

Reference Library
- Volumes of History
- Poetry / Literature
- Newspapers and Magazines

1149 Main Street
(Hwy. 7 at Cherry Brook Road)
Westphal, Halifax County
B2Z 1A8

(902) 434-6223
(902) 434-2306
Toll Free 1-800-465-0767 (in N.S.)

Auditorium
- Musical Events
- Theatre and Drama
- Religious Events
- Lectures / Seminars

Open Daily
Monday - Friday 9 a.m. - 5 p.m.
Saturday   10 a.m. 4 p.m.

Picture Brochure of the *Black Cultural Centre of Nova Scotia*

Photograph C: Courtesy of *Mrs. Beatrice (Johnson) Jackson*

Annie V. (Beals) Johnson, best friend of Mom Suse

Photograph D: Courtesy of *Vivian Willis*

Vivian Willis, grand-daughter of Mom Suse (dust jacket)

Footnotes

Chapter 1

1. <u>Drinking Isn't Indian</u>, National Native Alcohol and Drug Abuse Program, 1982, p. 23.

2. Ibid. p. 10.

3. <u>Mi'kmaw Resource Guide</u>, Eastern Woodland Publishing, 1997, p. 7.

4. Borrett, William, <u>East Coast Port And Other Tales Under the Old Town Clock</u>, The Imperial Publishing Company Limited, 1946, p. 83.

Chapter 2

5. Interview with Mrs. Beatrice Jackson, September, 2003

Chapter 5

6. <u>Proposal and Espousal</u>, Watt & Shenston Press, 1886, p. 366.

7. Ibid. p. 367.

Chapter 6

8. <u>Week-End Book 'Social Anthology'</u>, The Nonesuch Press, 926, p. 156

BIBLIOGRAPHIES

ABC's of the Human Body, Reader's Digest Association Inc. 1988

Borrett, William. *East Coast Port And Other Tales Under the Town Clock.* The Imperial Publishing 1946

Dent's Historical and Geographical Atlas, J.M. Dent & Sons (Canada) Ltd. 1962

Drinking Isn't Indian. National Native Alcohol and Drug Abuse Programs 1982

Fishbein's Illustrated Medical and Health Encyclopedia, Vol. 4, H.S. Stuttman Co. Inc. 1977

Funk & Wagnalls New Encyclopedia, Funk & Wagnall, Vol. 1, 1971 Company Limited 1946

The Golden Treasury of Knowledge, Vol. 2. Golden Press 1961

Halifax – Dartmouth Telephone Directory. Maritime Telegraph & Telephone Co. Limited 1944

History of the County of Pictou. Canadian Reprint Series No. 31, Mika Studio 1972

The Holy Bible, The King James Version

Hundley, Ian. Canada: *Immigrants & Settlers.* Gagg Publishing Limited 1980

Jackson, Beatrice V. *Interview* of September 2003

Jones, L.F. Canada, *The Maritime Provinces.* McGraw-Hill Company of Canada Limited, 1966

Laye, Camara. *L'enfant Noir* Maury-Eurolivres S.A.1953

The Merk's Manual of Diagnosis and Therapy, Merck Sharp & Dohme Research Laboratories

Martinello, I.L. *Call Us Canadians.* McGraw-Hill Ryerson 1978

Mi'kmaw Resource Guide, Eastern Woodland Publishing 1997

Proposal and Espousal. Watt & Shenston Press 1886

Regan, John W. *Sketches and Traditions of the Northwest Arm*, Halifax, Nova Scotia. Hounslow Press 1978

Sherwood, Roland H. *Pictou Pioneers.* Lancelot Press 1973

Week-End Book 'Social Anthology', The Nonesuch Press 1926

White, J. E. *The King's Daughter And Other Stories for Girls*, Southern Publishing Association, Tennessee 1910

Willis, Vivian. *Mom Suse.* Willis Productions 1994

Yarsinke, Amy Waters. *Bibliography: Norfolk's Church Street*, Between Memory & Reality Arcadia Publishing 1990

Newspapers and Articles

Adventist Review, Black History Month Tribute, February 1991

Cornwallis Street Baptist Church, Church History Information Sheet, Halifax 2000

Student News 2. Graham Creighton Junior High, Student Union, November 1972

The Black Cultural Centre for Nova Scotia, Black Biographies & Chronology

The Daily News, Great Eastern News Company Ltd., April 1985

The Halifax Herald, 'The Hindu Problem', Halifax Herald Limited, April 1914

The Halifax Herald, Halifax Herald Limited, August 1933

The Ladies' World, A Monthly Magazine, S.H. Moore Co., Publishers 1909

The Men's Brotherhood Community Program Recognition Dinner for Buddy Daye, Halifax 1990

The Preston Board of Trade, Tribute Night, 'Clyde Gray', May 1996

The Nova Scotia Museum, 'The Micmac', June 1985

The Nova Scotian, Halifax Herald Limited, June 1982

The Time Chronical, Cambridge, Ontario, August 1987

The Windsor Tribune, Nova Scotia, August 1947